*Few of us trust a write
bereavement who has not l
she writes of it with warmth, honesty and humanity.
The short chapters and the conversational style suit the
subject matter perfectly, and those who are feeling raw
from grief will find much comfort here.*
**Richard Littledale, Author and Broadcaster.
Author of Postcards From the Land of Grief: Comfort for
the Journey Through Loss Towards Hope.**

*In this emotional roller coaster of a book, Deacon Sylvie
holds your hand as she lays bare how the death and loss
of two husbands shapes her view of the world and her, at
times, fragile faith. A book that places honesty and
authenticity in place of mindless, glib cliché. A book that
becomes your friend and travels the lonely road with you.*
**Mark Dowd, Award-Winning
Religious Writer and Broadcaster.
Author of my Tsunami Journey:
The Quest for God in a Broken World**

*Those who have lost a beloved partner and soulmate
may find that even a lifelong Christian faith provides little
comfort. This book is for them. Sylvie Nicholls describes
experiences which make Biblical teachings about eternal
life feel concrete, fresh and tangible.
I found a lot here which chimes with me following the
death of my husband.*
Kristine Pommert, Award-Winning Radio Producer

Sylvie Nicholls takes us along the journey into the shadow of the death of a beloved partner. The highs and lows of this sacred time are witnessed through her personal recollections that may provide comfort to those who are also travelling a similar path of their own. Times of sadness and joy are interspersed with reassuring encounters with the 'other' which leave us knowing we are never alone on that narrow path.
Matt Arnold, Editor,
The Christian Parapsychologist Journal

A poignant evocation of Sylvie's experience as she deals with the illness and death of a loved one, providing glimpses into deeper realms of being via accounts of dreams, visions and episodes of synchronicity. The way Sylvie is able to weave poetry, metaphor and symbolism into her story serves to enrich it further. Importantly, it explores the possibility that, despite suffering, there is always hope: hope that, following death, rebirth is possible and that, eventually, the journey through loss and grief can be a 'growthful' one in which there is a deeper wisdom to be discovered and an ongoing life to be lived.
Darren Taylor, Counsellor and Psychotherapist

In 'Treasure on the Shore', Sylvie Nicholls deftly weaves together candid, honest encounters with grief alongside beautiful, heart-warming poetry, to accompany our own reflections and resourcing. The blend of reporting and reflecting really draws us in, allowing her words to touch the strands of grief in our own lives. A true companion on our own journey of life and faith.
Revd. Phil Gough, Chair, Lancashire District, Methodist Church

The Treasure On the Shore

Copyright © 2022 Sylvie Nicholls

The moral right of the author has been asserted.

Apart from any fair dealing for the purposes of research or private study, or criticism or review, as permitted under Copyright, Deign and Patents Act 1998, this publication may only be reproduced, stored or transmitted, in any form or by any means, with prior permission in writing of the publishers, or in any case of the reprographic reproduction in accordance with the terms of licences issued by the Copyright Licensing Agency. Enquiries concerning reproduction outside these terms should be sent to the publishers.

PublishU Ltd

www.publishu.com

Scripture taken from the Holy Bible, New King James Version, © 1982 by Thomas Nelson, Inc. All rights reserved.

Scripture taken from the Holy Bible, New International Version, © 1973, 1978, 1984 by International Bible Society. Used by permission of Hodder & Stoughton, a member of the Hodder Headline Group. All rights reserved.

Scripture taken from the Holy Bible, New Living Translation, copyright © 1996, 2004, 2007 by Tyndale House Foundation. Used by permission of Tyndale House Publishers, Inc., Carol Stream, IL 60188. All rights reserved.

Acknowledgement

I am grateful to all those who have encouraged me on this journey, through bereavement and then to putting pen to paper in the form of this book. In writing it, I have been especially blessed by coaching from Matt Bird and from the constant support of my husband, Robert. Thanks also to Jennifer Willis for the cover art.

I am so thankful for what I have learned from the bereaved over many years, and, especially, for all I learned about life, death, love and courage from two special men: Raymond Thomas Williams and James Edwin Phillips.

This book is dedicated to my son, Michael Phillips.

Contents

Foreword

Introduction

Chapter 1 The Change of Life

Chapter 2 La-La Land

Chapter 3 'There's something there'

Chapter 4 Let this Cup Pass

Chapter 5 Good News or Bad News?

Chapter 6 Traffic Light Tears

Chapter 7 Strawberry Moments

Chapter 8 The illness is not the person

Chapter 9 When you haven't got a prayer

Chapter 10 Behind the smile

Chapter 11 Things could be worse

Chapter 12 Human Kindness

Chapter 13 Shall we talk about death?

Chapter 14 Dreams and Visions

Chapter 15 Meltdown

Chapter 16 Thoughts which Taunt

Chapter 17 Checking Out

Chapter 18 Seeking Shelter

Chapter 19 Surprised by Joy

Chapter 20	The Day After
Chapter 21	Finding my Still
Chapter 22	Healed Beyond the World
Chapter 23	Where's my happy ending?
Chapter 24	To tell or not to tell
Chapter 25	Could I have done more?
Chapter 26	Parting with Possessions
Chapter 27	Life after Life
Chapter 28	The Precious Gift of Presence
Chapter 29	Starting from Here
Chapter 30	Love after Loss
Epilogue	

Foreword

There are some people who come into your life that are a gift in themselves. For me, Sylvie is one of those people. Since first meeting her when she was appointed as one of the ministers at my home church, her wit, wisdom, compassion and ability to be in the moment with you have been a source of joy and support to me for nigh on thirty years. During this time, I have also observed her walking alongside the broken and the broken-hearted and then helping others to do the same. Out of her ministry and her lived experience, much wisdom has been accumulated. Now it is time for that to be shared more widely.

While no one can give us all the answers as to how to walk with grief and loss, when those who have been there share their stories, we find comfort in shared experience and fresh insights that seem to glint in the darkness. There are many such glinting treasures to be found in Sylvie's story. We travel with her through the darkest of times, yet it is hope infused. I smiled, I cried, I laughed out loud and I paused in wonder at the moments of heaven touching earth.

Sylvie has always had a way with words. Words that flow off the page with such earthy reality and yet are interlaced with poetic beauty. Words that offer images, phrases and rhythms which give voice to the inexpressible. Phrases like 'strawberry moments' which can give us permission to enjoy the glimpse of light in the darkness and a way to recognise, label and hold onto those moments when they arise.

Words that hold you safe, words that offer healing and words that offer hope.

The journey through the *'wilderness of grief'*, where we are shaken to our very core, is often one of just getting through each day, each hour, each moment. We all will travel this road of grief and loss at times in our lives. Some who read this book are on this road currently, some are looking back and seeing how far they have travelled and some are keen to know how to travel with others on this road. Some may have been intrigued by the title and topic and will be surprised how it equips them to travel this road in the future.

This is a book that has treasures for everyone; for those who know Jesus, those of other faiths and for those who have no faith. It is a book for those who are just hoping there is more to this life than that which they have experienced so far. As you read, if you find yourself drawn to a particular phrase or passage, take a moment and let it drop into your spirit...it may be a treasure to store up deep within you for your own journey through this life.

Alison Bryan, Co-ordinator of Healing Ministry, Methodist Central Hall, Westminster, London, UK

Introduction

You can either be a victim of the world or an adventurer in search of treasure. It all depends on how you view your life.

- Paulo Coelho

'Lightning never strikes twice!' Well, that's what they say. Sitting alone in the familiar surroundings of the church where I worked as a minister, I felt it had struck twice. Silent tears trickled down my face, startling a colleague who happened to walk in at that moment. Phil listened patiently as I poured it all out, how that day's date — 30th June — was the 30th anniversary of the death of my first husband, Ray. When I was 28, Ray had been diagnosed with bladder cancer and passed away ten months later. That day, I was seeking a few quiet moments to remember him, and our short but happy life together. Now, I was facing the likelihood of my second husband, Jim, dying within months from another form of cancer: an aggressive brain tumour.

'I can't believe this is happening again!' I cried. All the pain of that first bereavement had come flooding back that day. I dreaded having to undertake a similar kind of journey toward what now seemed the inevitable, ghastly outcome: widowhood for a second time. It was a journey I had no will or energy to face.

Many people have undertaken similar journeys by the side of loved ones. Forced to look on, as someone they care deeply about reels from a terminal diagnosis, a life-limiting verdict hanging over their heads. The afflicted person might linger for months, or years, but for all involved it is like living under the Sword of Damocles. Over the last thirty years in my role as a minister, it has been my privilege to offer pastoral support to many living through such a nightmare. Even though I have first-hand experience of what it is like, I learned long ago never to use the words 'I know how you feel' because each of us is unique in our experience and it is better to listen to how things are in someone's own words.

So why this book? This kind of writing often has a therapeutic purpose for the author, and writing things down is a useful exercise to help anyone process past painful events. But by writing now, eight years after Jim died, my perspective has widened beyond the intensity of grief I experienced in those first years. Perhaps I might best explain it using an analogy based on rock tumbling.

My first husband, Ray, tried his hand at a whole host of hobbies, in each of which he reached a reasonable level of proficiency before moving on to the next thing which piqued his interest. Once, he became fascinated by rock tumbling. Off he would go to a beach to search for 'treasure', taking no equipment with him (a craze for treasure hunting using a metal detector came later). Ray would walk up and down the beach, patiently scanning the shoreline for any ordinary looking pebbles which might turn out to be gemstones in disguise.

THE TREASURE ON THE SHORE

One day, I watched as he picked up a grubby little brown stone, turned it over and over in his fingers and grinned broadly.

Back home, into the rock tumbler machine it went, along with a mixture of other stones, water and grit which would serve to knock it into shape. The little machine whirred round and round for days, smoothing and polishing its contents; irritating me with its constant background rumble. To my surprise, when it was emptied, the grubby little stone had been transformed into a shiny translucent one: a small but beautiful piece of amber. Ray would add settings to the stones he polished, turning them into pieces of jewellery he could gift to myself and others.

'The Treasure on the Shore' is a bit like that stone. Grief has been described as something which hits us in waves. After each tsunami of emotions assaults us, we begin to regain our balance when another wave hits, knocking us off our feet and threatening to pull us under. Both before and after we lose a loved one, torrents of grief bombard our spirit. Whenever and however those waves recede, what might be left behind on the shoreline of our lives? Like a beach full of bland pebbles, what is left may appear at first very ordinary, not worthy of special notice. When we take a mental walk along the shoreline of grief and more closely examine these stones, they act like 'memory stones', flashing snapshots into our minds of scenes from our experience, some of which can be very painful to relive.

This book holds 'memory stones' drawn from my own experience: episodes from the final earthly journeys of Ray, and especially Jim, but also draws on my years as a minister involved in pastoral care of the bereaved. It seeks to look at such stones not as something to be discarded as being no longer of value, but as something which, with time and patience, might just be transformed into something beautiful. Like a piece of amber in a rock tumbler, our lives might be shaken to the core before something beautiful is revealed — but once we discover that treasure, it warms and inspires us. What is more, we come to realise we can hold out some of the treasure we have discovered as a gift to another, in the hope it will warm and inspire them also.

Within these pages, I sift through the grubby brown stones in the hope of glimpsing some radiant jewel within. I invite you, the reader, to join me in this exploration, in the fervent hope that you might recognise something which resonates with your own experience of loss. There is no 'right' or 'wrong' way to grieve, but I have found that, whenever and wherever one person's experience mirrors and ministers to another's, we are moved to recognise our common humanity and feel less alone.

The snapshots in these pages include poems I composed during and after the passing of Jim. My pen turned to telling the story in poetic prose whenever the emotion I was experiencing at the time felt too fierce or raw to be expressed in any other way.

THE TREASURE ON THE SHORE

Believing at the time that these were for my eyes only, I found them cathartic, not least because I was learning more and more about how emotional pain needs to be confronted and tolerated as much as we can bear, rather than suppressed. If we try to deny our pain, or distance ourselves with constant distractions, the tide of grief may recede, but like a tsunami, sooner or later it returns with greater force. It is my hope and prayer that something in these pages will set you on the path towards discovering what might be your own treasure on the shore, or assist you as you seek to help others discover theirs.

SYLVIE NICHOLLS

Dialogue with Grief

Grief can come in waves they say,
Its currents cold as death:
My head's been under for so long
I'm gasping for my breath!
Its agony unbidden comes
To rampage through my mind;
I must admit no saving grace
In its foul ranks I find!

I ask: Are you some demon
Bringing chaos in your wake?
Who urges me to give up hope,
And life itself forsake?
Have you ripped scars in my spirit
That time will not erase?
Can your devilish mode of torture
Hold anything of Grace?

I know not! – Yet, I also know,
There is nothing to be gained

THE TREASURE ON THE SHORE

By denying your existence:
That I must not run from pain.
For here, within your black abyss,
Angels reach to cradle me
As once they ministered to Christ
In dark Gethsemane.

Today, Grief, I am not alone!
But girded up by faith,
I dare accept your summons and
Confront you face to face...
If I tolerate your torrents
Even as they're drowning me,
What treasure will be left behind
By your receding sea?

So Yes, you may engulf me, Grief,
But you must promise this:
That some legacy of wisdom
Will be your parting gift...

SYLVIE NICHOLLS

Chapter 1

The Change of Life

People have often shared with me how much they detest change. Usually, they mean some change which, in their opinion, is a change for the worse; this might refer to anything from objecting to a different coffee being served after worship, to irritation about a political decision which impacts them in some way. They tell me the worst changes to adapt to are those situations where they feel they have no control over, or choice in the matter.

So many people, never more so since Covid, have known that moment... That precise, earth-shattering moment when you realise normal life as you know it is turned inside out. Vestiges of it remain, but everything is somehow tinged, tainted, with a new reality you really don't want to be living in, or living through. When you realise there may be no way back.

Normality for me, on a bright Spring morning in March 2014, was a Conference Centre where I had travelled to serve on a committee interviewing would-be ministers. We were very aware of the awesome, precious privilege entrusted to us, assisting each candidate to discern whether ordination was part of their future, or whether God might have other plans in store for them. Each day began with worship and that morning had included PowerPoint slides illustrating the story of Jesus being tempted in the wilderness. Powerful, moving images flashed up on the screen before us.

SYLVIE NICHOLLS

One of these depicted a clearly exhausted Jesus being physically held up on both sides by ministering angels. As I gazed at that image, I was seized, quite inexplicably, by an overpowering sadness. I did not realise how soon that kind of feeling would manifest itself in my life as an almost daily reality or how quickly I would stand in need of that same kind of angelic ministration to get me through each day.

The next morning, I was called out of a small sub-panel by an urgent summons. A chaplain informed me that someone had rung the centre asking to speak to me. I realised it must be something serious for the matter not to be postponed until I was free. My heart galloped as fast as my mind as I took the call. As far as I knew, my husband Jim would have gone to work that morning as usual, driving a distance of about 18 miles to the school where he worked as a teaching assistant. His work in the classroom supporting students with special needs was as much a vocation for him as my role as a minister was for me. Having really struggled at school himself, often falling behind, he had a natural instinct about how to bring out the best in any students who might feel similarly. If a student expressed an interest in football, he would happily chat about their team and goal scoring to cajole them into learning arithmetic. It was no surprise to me when students voted him their favourite teaching assistant. But it wasn't all plain sailing: sometimes he would come home nursing a bruise, because he had had to intervene when a student lost control and decided to attack another student or a teacher.

THE TREASURE ON THE SHORE

At six feet tall and of solid stature, Jim could stop any aggressor in their tracks by positioning himself between them and their intended victim; something the teachers often expressed appreciation for. Jim never resented the students involved in these incidents. He understood their challenges and was concerned to find ways to take the heat out of a situation and provide the best learning experience.

All of this ran through my mind as I listened to the voice of Jim's headteacher on the phone. I tried to still a gnawing sense of dread as she explained the reason for her call. An ambulance had been summoned and Jim had been rushed to hospital. Had he been attacked by a student? The cause was much more bizarre. A colleague Jim had been car-sharing with had arrived at school that morning in a state of great distress. Jim had been exhibiting strange behaviour driving to work. In fact, he had terrified his poor colleague due to his erratic driving and apparent inability to respond to her pleas for caution. The head added that staff had remarked recently on how Jim seemed to lose concentration in lessons and appear withdrawn at times. None of this sounded like the man I knew and loved, a gentle giant with an outgoing personality. Withdrawn was certainly not a word anyone who knew Jim would normally attach to him.

My hands trembled as I rang the hospital number the head had given me. I discovered that they, the health professionals, were as much in the dark as I was to know what could possibly be wrong with Jim. Doctors had given him the once over and concluded there was no need for any further action. Could I come and collect him?

SYLVIE NICHOLLS

I explained I was 200 miles away, but would endeavour to arrange assistance. Thankfully, my closest ministry colleague Phil was very willing to help. While Phil set off for the hospital I set off for home. The drive, though I have driven longer distances, somehow seemed to me the longest, hardest journey of my entire life. Forcing myself to concentrate on the road ahead, I could not quieten a persistent voice in my head, which told me; warned me, it seemed, that nothing was ever going to be the same again. Somehow, I knew this for a fact, yet I did not want to acknowledge it. I needed my precious, cosy normality to linger a little while longer before it threatened to be snatched away.

THE TREASURE ON THE SHORE

Homeward Bound

I can't shake off this nameless dread;

This journey seems the longest time,

Yet the quickest time to travel too -

From what has been, to what will be

Toward a very different 'you'.

SYLVIE NICHOLLS

Chapter 2
La-la Land

La-la Land: A notional place characterised by fantasy, self-absorption and blissful lack of touch with reality.

- www.phrases.org.uk

The acrid stench of burning hit me as soon as I entered the house. What on earth was going on? By the time I arrived home, Jim had been on his own for a couple of hours after my colleague had to leave. At first nothing seemed amiss. He greeted me as normal, though seeming somewhat subdued. I experienced a strange sense of unreality mixed with relief: I wanted to pretend so badly that everything was fine and dandy. But of course, it couldn't be. Jim must have had some sort of weird breakdown to drive so crazily, and I wouldn't be here at home if all was well.

I tried to locate the source of the smell. 'I'm cooking dinner,' Jim explained with a grin. He was a good, if basic, cook. His cooking dinner should be no cause for alarm — until I investigated what was actually in the oven. A large potato sat next to a single, unpeeled carrot. They were perched not on a normal oven tray but atop a round, brightly decorated tray which Jim was fond of eating his meals off. It bore the 'Guinness' logo. He loved both the logo and the drink itself!

Normally, I knew he would never have made this error; the enamelled surface of the tray beneath the charred vegetables was now blistered and damaged beyond repair. On the worktop nearby, I noticed a kitchen towel with a hole burned clean through the middle. Jim, however, was blissfully oblivious. Stilling my rising panic, I set about making us a meal, settled Jim down for the night and wondered what on earth the morrow would bring.

The next morning, I woke with a start after a fitful night. At first, I was unsure of where I was, having been due to spend most of the week at the Conference Centre. As I came round, I allowed myself to indulge for a few minutes in the fantasy of 'life as it ought to be right now'. I had been really looking forward to the weekend when Jim, our son Michael and I were due to celebrate Mothering Sunday with a meal out. Would that even happen now? The world of ordinary things seemed suddenly a closed book. I roused myself, and was relieved to hear Jim's quiet, ordered breathing beside me. What would this day bring to shake our world?

With some persuasion I managed to get Jim to the doctor that morning, where I voiced my concerns. The doctor promised to follow up on the results of tests from the hospital and spoke of a possible CAT scan. He did not seem unduly concerned, assuring us it could be anything from a psychiatric episode due to stress, diabetes or even a mini-stroke. I came away feeling guilty about any stress Jim might have been experiencing due to a forthcoming move in connection with my ministry, yet I felt he had been handling it well until that point.

THE TREASURE ON THE SHORE

To take Jim's mind off his worries, we took a short walk that afternoon to his favourite café. There was a charity shop next door into which he suggested we pop before eating. I was heartened to see his interest in everyday things being revived, and into the shop we went. As I stood idly rifling through a clothes rail I glanced across to where Jim was standing in the toy section, which puzzled me because our son was too old for such things and no grandchildren were on the horizon.

Jim's attention was transfixed by a brightly coloured toy he was holding, turning it over and over again in his hands. It was a jack-in-the-box type toy for young children. The kind where you pressed one of four buttons and a figure would pop up. Over and over again he was pressing those buttons, looking strangely bemused whenever the bright little figure inside popped up to greet him.

As I watched, I began to fear Jim's focus on this object was not so much interest as obsession. In the end, I had to gently wrestle it from him. It was as if he could barely stand to leave it behind as we left the shop. I pondered this over lunch in the café next door. Was my dear husband's mind disintegrating right in front of me? When we had finished eating, I rose from my seat and made for the door, expecting him to follow. But he remained rooted to the spot, a benign grin spreading across his features. 'Come on love, time to go,' I encouraged. No response. As I stood by the door beckoning him over, I became aware of other eyes looking on. Expressions which seemed to me to convey: 'Leave the poor guy alone, he wants to stay where he is.'

Eventually, I had to physically tug Jim from his seat and manoeuvre him through the doorway, conscious of disapproving glances all round. As I bundled him into the car I wanted to go home, shut the door — and shut the whole world out.

Chapter 3

'There's Something There'

Early morning email to my colleague Phil:

Jim sent a number of bizarre text messages to me last night - probably to others too, as one person rang me at 12.30 this morning and half scared me to death as I thought it was the hospital. God knows what we will find out today.

After I reported Jim's increasingly bizarre behaviour to his GP, he was admitted to hospital urgently for tests. On the second evening there, I arrived to find he had been moved to another ward and seemed totally bewildered. His stuff had been dumped in a bag on the bed and he seemed unable to sort anything or work out what was happening. I kept praying that we would soon be given answers, that 'whatever-this-is' was curable; that my precious husband would soon recover. I longed to get back the Jim who was normally so upbeat, full of humour and life.

Next day, a young doctor approached Jim's bed as I sat beside him. Carefully drawing the curtains around the bed, the doctor regarded us with a solemn expression. He appeared fidgety, on edge. I braced myself for what he might be about to reveal, for I sensed he had no more wish to be there at that moment than we had. This was not going to be good news.

SYLVIE NICHOLLS

As the doctor explained the results of a scan on Jim's brain, I became mesmerised by the faded pattern on the hospital curtain framing his head. It was as if my mind was trying to escape the confines of my body and find comfort in the banally trivial. There was a 'tumour like' thing in Jim's skull, he was explaining. 'There's something there!' As he said this, he pointed to each side of his own head. His gestures only served to increase the crushing weight his words were having on my spirit. We could no longer deny something was badly wrong with Jim. We were being forced to leave La-La Land and confront a terrible new reality.

THE TREASURE ON THE SHORE

After the Scan

'There's something there,' the doctor says,
And gestures to the right. And left!
Side of his head.
(His own head, not my love's)
Framed by the faded curtains round the bed.

He looks so pale!
I sense that he would rather be
Anywhere, in any company,
Than standing here, delivering
This verdict right in front of me.

What is this 'something' —
But he will not be drawn,
Just hints how further tests will tell.
Yet I can tell already:
We are headed into hell.

SYLVIE NICHOLLS

Chapter 4
Let This Cup Pass

Round Robin email:

The change in Jim after the medication has kicked in is remarkable. From the day before, when he could not feed or wash himself, he is back to the 'old Jim' so I thank God for that. It means we can have a two-way conversation and he can begin to understand what has happened to him. At the moment he looks like the fittest patient on Ward 21, up and dressed and phoning people! It is his birthday today (he is used to the April Fool jokes) so I am taking Michael over to see him again. Mike was upset the other day seeing his dad so poorly but said our friend Paul 'cheered me up' giving him a lift home.

Jim came into this world on Easter Sunday 1956. That date also happened to be 1st April, a less positive association, of course: he was teased at school for being an 'April Fool'. Now, 58 years later, and a week after his collapse, we marked, rather than celebrated, the occasion in hospital. Jim was in good spirits, optimistic that he would soon be on the mend.

A few weeks later, I attended an Easter Sunday service at church. By then, neurosurgeons had cut into one side of Jim's head, to try to find out what was really going on inside his brain. It had left behind an ugly scar, pinned with staples.

Afterwards, they informed us that this first biopsy had not yielded enough information to make an accurate diagnosis and they would have to cut through the other side of his skull, as well. This time they made a 'bigger hole,' they told us afterwards. Yes, anyone could see that, from the additional nine ugly staples crossing his bare scalp on that side, pinching the wound together. These procedures had left just a little of his hair stubbornly clinging on to his scalp at the back of his head. I could not look at it without feeling a mixture of revulsion and nostalgia. I used to tease Jim that his hair was his finest physical asset: thick and white. I had loved to run my fingers through it. Now his scalp appeared so sore, so wounded; yet he bore it all with a quiet, resigned dignity.

As I sat in church that Easter day, a picture flashed into my mind from some years before: me walking into a Crematorium Chapel where I regularly conducted funerals. I noticed something odd about the large brass cross which always stood on the table at the front. Whenever I had previously visited, it had presented from the front view as a rather beautiful but bare cross. A bare cross symbolises Christ risen from the dead and was traditionally used at Protestant funerals in the chapel. On this occasion, the cross was standing sideways on and, for the first time, I realised that on the other side was an intricately carved figure of Christ on the cross; the traditional presentation for Roman Catholic funerals.

As I had waited there, about to welcome a family arriving for a service of committal, I thought about which of these faces of the Cross might actually speak to them most that day, in their place of deep grief.

THE TREASURE ON THE SHORE

Would it be the plain cross, symbolising the triumph of Christ over death and, therefore, the hope of heaven for their loved one, or would it be the broken body of Christ, depicted in the throes of the agony of earthly suffering. A crematorium employee entered at that point, walked up to the Cross and turned the plain side outermost, the suffering Christ once again hidden from view. I felt a pang of sadness because something was telling me that when we grieve, we need to hold both these images in heart and mind; to know that blessed hope of the life to come but, also, we need to know that Christ is there suffering with us, just where we are, right in the midst of our pain.

Now, here I was, part of the congregation celebrating Easter: Christ risen, triumphant over evil and death. Normally as a minister, I could not wait to celebrate the joys of Easter Sunday after the comparative bleakness of the Lent season, but that day was different. Only the suffering, dying Christ on the Cross could speak to me just then, or help me to cling to any sense that ministering angels were still holding me up just as they had strengthened him in the desert.

Good Friday that year had been Michael's 21st birthday, but with his dad so ill in hospital, no one had felt like celebrating. As the organist struck up the first notes of a triumphant Easter hymn, I could not help but think there would be fresh horrors to endure. I had no stomach that day to entertain the celebratory hymns of Easter. Instead, I recalled the words of a hymn we often sang on Good Friday: 'O sacred head, sore wounded.'

SYLVIE NICHOLLS

It vividly describes the crucified Christ, mocked by a crown of sharp thorns forced on to his head, dying slowly and painfully from his wounds. Easter Day it may have been, but my spirit was still hanging out in the Garden of Gethsemane, desperately praying there with Jesus: 'Let this cup pass!'

THE TREASURE ON THE SHORE

O Sacred Head

'O sacred head, sore wounded'
We sang in church today:
Then I thought of your head, my love,
So wounded in its way...

Not by a crown of spiteful thorns
But staples, crudely placed,
To hide the wounds you'd carried:
The cross you'd had to face.

No anaesthetic for our Lord
As thorns pierced skin and flesh!
Yet, like Him, you would bear the scars
And love God nonetheless.

Your head, so sorely wounded,
I saw in vision blessed
Laid on the Saviour's shoulder
And entering his rest.

SYLVIE NICHOLLS

And as he cradled your dear head
I thought I heard him say
Your suffering, too, is sanctified -
Because of Easter Day.

THE TREASURE ON THE SHORE

Chapter 5

Good News or Bad News?

Round Robin email:

The good news is that they managed to get the results they needed from the second op and Jim does not have to go through surgery again for that. Also, they believe it is treatable. The bad news is that they say the treatment for this kind of tumour is itself very aggressive and life-threatening. There will be a regime of chemotherapy followed by radiotherapy. He will have to go into hospital for a week of chemo, then home for two weeks. This cycle repeats itself four times — if he survives, they will go ahead with radiotherapy.

As the drama continued to play out in front of me, I desperately wanted to be able to send friends and family better news, but it was a rather mixed missive I typed in a 'round robin' email setting out his prognosis. As I had started to compose it, I felt like I was asking each recipient: 'Do you want the good news or the bad news?' Jim was suffering an advanced Primary Central Nervous System Lymphoma. A rare and aggressive form of non-Hodgkin lymphoma, cancer cells grow in the brain or spinal cord. It was about as far from good news as one could get.

SYLVIE NICHOLLS

We embarked on a nightmarish merry-go-round of stays in hospital interspersed with a few days at home, lurching from crisis to crisis. Jim had to be constantly monitored in case his condition suddenly altered. My work pattern shifted to what could be managed from home, such as phoning church members rather than visiting. Inevitably, some people I was contacting to offer pastoral support ended up feeling like they should support me; something I appreciated but which also made me realise how exhausting it is repeating the story of someone's illness over and over. I came to wish I had a taped message I could play each time someone kindly inquired, ' How's Jim doing this week?' One member of a group of older ladies, who Jim had often sat with after Sunday services, asked, 'When's Jim coming back? We really miss his stories!' So do I, I thought, so do I!

Each time Jim underwent chemotherapy there was a chance he would not bounce back from it, and it began to badly affect his kidneys. Regular blood tests were essential to monitor his blood counts in case he suddenly needed a lifesaving transfusion. This requirement led to an incident which was to badly shake my faith in the system. Who knew how dangerous a Friday could be in the grand scheme of things? Or, at least, in the National Health Service's grand scheme of things. For Friday teeters on the brink of the 'weekend', which means reduced availability of even the most basic services one might expect to receive when undergoing the kind of treatment Jim needed simply to stay alive.

THE TREASURE ON THE SHORE

On the Friday in question, Jim and I were enjoying lunch in a pub close to the hospital; it was just before we were due to meet with his consultant. We were also waiting anxiously for news we hoped would be of a different nature to that we were getting used to reeling from lately. Our son Michael was about to get the results of his university course. What a struggle it had been for him, completing his Mathematics degree while his father had been so ill. Michael had bravely insisted we tell no one at his university about the situation, but Jim had been so worried about the effect it might have on his studies. To his great credit, Michael had got his head down and persevered. The call came through, and we celebrated over the phone with an excited Michael announcing he had gained a good result.

Good news tastes all the sweeter when your life is full of the opposite. We were overjoyed and unaware that our high spirits were soon about to crash back to earth again. It wasn't so much what the consultant said to us that day which shocked us — but what we overheard him say to another person. He was an excellent consultant, we thought; a dedicated professional. Perhaps a little too cheerful at times (I worried) as once I had realised there was little chance of Jim's recovery, he seemed to still be promising a happy outcome.

As we sat in his office that afternoon, he studied Jim's recent blood results and frowned: they would need to keep a close eye on those over the weekend, he explained. The number of platelets in Jim's blood was rapidly falling, a side-effect of the chemo.

He wanted him to have another blood test the next morning and then he might require a transfusion. In the meantime, we must report back immediately if he had any bleeding episodes, like a nose bleed. This blood test would be vital to ensure the situation did not become critical. We could see that this requirement concerned him but we were not sure why. Surely the hospital was not closed over the weekend and the test would be a routine matter?

He asked us to wait a moment while he moved into an adjoining office to arrange the test in a phone call. Perhaps he did not realise the door was not fully closed and we could hear every word. We could not help but listen as he spoke the words forcefully over the phone: 'I've kept him alive for this long. I don't want him dying over the weekend!'

This was the first time he had used the word 'die' in our hearing. Jim's face was ashen, struggling to take it all in. On my part, I was experiencing a strange mixture of anger and disbelief. My faith in a system I thought would do everything it could to protect Jim was being shaken to the core. As I listened to this man trying to persuade whoever he was speaking to of the urgency of his request, I resolved that, if necessary, I would just turn up with Jim at A&E that weekend and demand that they do a blood test. Eventually, the consultant managed to obtain agreement that Jim could visit one of the wards the following day and receive the test.

As we set off for home, I was struggling inwardly: should I be mad at the system, which includes so many hard-working professionals giving their all for the NHS?

THE TREASURE ON THE SHORE

Or should I be angry about the obvious lack of resources being provided in order for these professionals to be able to get on with their jobs, finding fulfilment and satisfaction in what most believe to be their vocation: saving lives instead of being forced to beg for what they need in order to do so? I came down in favour of the latter.

SYLVIE NICHOLLS

Blood Count

You will need another blood count,
That is what I recommend —
The problem, is you'll need it
Within this next weekend.

We listen as he pleads our case
With fervour on the phone
(Through his door that is half open)
And each word's hitting home.

Don't let him die this weekend!
I've kept him alive this long!
Test his blood and then assess it
To prevent things going wrong.

Meanwhile our world's imploding
For I just can't understand
How your life is now dependent
On the pleas of this one man.

THE TREASURE ON THE SHORE

For a blood test on a weekend —
For someone to oversee
If things might be going badly:
Or else? Fatality?

Without a simple blood count
Your life could now be lost —
And maybe only then they
Would count up the real cost.

SYLVIE NICHOLLS

THE TREASURE ON THE SHORE

Chapter 6
Traffic Light Tears

There is a sacredness in tears. They are not the mark of weakness, but of power. They speak more eloquently than ten thousand tongues. They are the messengers of overwhelming grief, of deep contrition, and of unspeakable love.

- Washington Irving

At the end of evening visiting in hospital, I would kiss Jim goodbye and walk through the labyrinth of corridors to the car park. To any onlooker, I looked not much different to any other casual visitor to the wards. If, as human beings, our outward appearance instead depicted what was happening within our spirits, I might have been seen hobbling along, dragging my feet, looking like I might collapse at any moment under the weight of a huge rucksack on my back. I would have been surrounded by other departing visitors, bearing similar or even larger loads on their backs.

For me, I was acutely conscious of a weight of sadness I was carrying not just for myself but for Jim and our son. The route between the hospital in the city and our home in a nearby town involved much stopping and starting at seemingly endless sets of traffic lights. On one such journey, as the car slowed down to halt at a red light, I could not prevent a rush of tears.

SYLVIE NICHOLLS

As the lights changed through amber to green, I chided myself to focus on the road ahead. But from then on, this crying at traffic lights became a regular habit. Here, at least, was a safe place to give in to my feelings. I did not want to get upset at Jim's bedside. Likewise, I did not want to arrive home to greet my son looking flustered and stressed. There may not have been exactly twenty traffic lights between hospital and home, but it certainly felt like it.

Travelling to and from the bedside of a loved one poses challenges, depending on many factors, such as the location, the availability of public transport or offers of lifts; where to park and at what cost when you get there. I had listened to such frustrations being shared in conversation many times. If the journey involves visiting someone in a serious condition, the emotional toll it took on the person was clearly very great. It was not only a struggle at times to get there, but also to sit for endless hours by the bedside, perhaps desperately trying to shore up the mood of the patient whilst trying not to lose control of your own. If the patient is unable to engage much, it can be quite a tedious, at times soul-destroying, pursuit.

When someone shared such difficulties, I could see how they might be struggling not to break down in front of me, just as they may have struggled at the bedside shortly before. Sometimes, though, people confided how giving in to tears had brought blessed relief, especially if they had somewhere to cry privately as they did not want to alarm others. I admired such courage, whilst at the same time thinking how lonely that must feel.

THE TREASURE ON THE SHORE

There were times with Jim when I would need to travel to the hospital to visit most days of the week, trying to find somewhere to grab a bite between afternoon and evening visiting hours so I didn't have to make the journey home in the heat of the rush hour and back again. How I wished there was a sci-fi device I could walk into at one end and be instantly transported to the haven of home at the other. Whilst I did believe such visits were a bit of a lifeline for Jim, and I wanted to be there, I would leave the ward at night with a heavy, sinking feeling that we were always teetering on the brink, and that things could go very badly wrong at any time. Carers relate similar feelings of exhaustion, emotional and physical. You both long for home and yet dread it, because returning there reminds you so vividly of the loss of your loved one's presence in the place you would most regularly enjoy it.

I learned to accept 'traffic light tears' as precious time. Tears are nothing to be ashamed of...in fact, they can be a relief, a release and a catalyst for healing. When training pastoral visitors, I had sometimes quoted the story of the little boy who observed a little girl after she had tripped in the school playground and scraped her knee. She sat on some steps and sobbed. The little boy sat beside her and cried with her, thus acknowledging and sharing in her pain. We might feel we must try to protect others through crying only when we are alone. It is a precious gift to us when someone is able to simply sit beside us in our sadness. Our gift to them may be allowing them to be there.

SYLVIE NICHOLLS

Twenty Traffic Lights

There must be twenty traffic lights
Betwixt His Bed and Home,
And, as the city greets the night,
I travel on, alone.

And when the light reverts to red
I stop, and sigh, and sigh...
But sometimes as the sighing stops
With head in hands, I cry.

The lights relentlessly will change
Through red and gold to green;
Then GO! — To What? To Where? I ask —
He is not there with me!

A safe world this, 'twixt Bed and Home
Where I can shed these tears:
Where I need not make others sad,
Nor add to others' fears.

THE TREASURE ON THE SHORE

There must be twenty traffic lights

Betwixt His Bed and Home:

And I have wept at every one,

And travelled on, alone.

SYLVIE NICHOLLS

THE TREASURE ON THE SHORE

Chapter 7

Strawberry Moments

A man walking in the wild comes across a tiger. He tries to run away, but the tiger chases him to the edge of a cliff. With no other means of escape, he resorts to climbing down a vine hanging over the edge. Halfway down the vine, clinging on with all his might, he stops to draw breath. To his horror he then spots, waiting at the base of the cliff, another tiger. There is no way out and the vine is not strong enough to hold his weight for long. Looking around, he notices that near the vine there is a plump red strawberry growing out of the rock. Reaching out, he picks the strawberry and eats it slowly, determined to savour each delicious bite.

Giggling with my girlfriends, rifling through racks of clothes in the busy shopping centre, we were making fun of the latest fashion trends. Holding up a bright orange jumpsuit one teased me: 'What about this for your next preaching appointment?' 'Never in a month of Sundays!' I laughed in reply. As we walked round and chatted, I felt myself relax and begin to feel 'normal' for the first time since Jim had been taken ill a few months before. This, I mused inwardly, was most definitely a 'strawberry moment'.

SYLVIE NICHOLLS

If you are someone who tries to offer help and support to others in times of difficulty, it is no bad thing to be reminded that there are times when it is important to graciously accept such support. As a minister, my role involved offering pastoral care. But as Jim's health worsened, my ability to offer that care was inevitably affected; my mind too crammed with personal concerns to help someone reflect upon their own. My colleagues shielded me as much as possible, undertaking extra duties themselves. Funerals or counselling the bereaved were off limits; I could not trust myself not to break down in front of a grieving family. Church members were gentle and supportive as they encouraged both Jim and I to keep going. Many of them knew and loved Jim. I was conscious they were grieving with us and for us. One of them, Mabel, shared with me the 'strawberry story'. I had heard variations of the story before, but this time it hit home.

I remembered how, when Ray was ill and confined to home, I had spent every moment away from him, whether at work or walking around a supermarket, beside myself with worry. For me to find joy in anything seemed almost a betrayal of the horrific circumstances he was facing. If I caught myself laughing at a funny story from a work colleague, I would inwardly scold myself for forgetting about the plight he was in, even for a moment.

Now, hearing the strawberry story, something within me seemed to be giving me permission (if I needed it) to be kinder towards myself in the present.

THE TREASURE ON THE SHORE

The lesson it carried seemed to be a need to learn how to savour the present moment, when the present moment is good, without allowing it to be completely spoiled by the wider circumstances we may find ourselves in. The key seems to be in 'allowing' ourselves to enjoy such moments, without guilt that we are finding any joy in them. There will always be an underlying current of anxiety in our spirits when we are accompanying a loved one through terrible times, but if we can recognise and savour 'strawberry moments' when they present themselves, they can help us remember that, despite everything, life can be good and there is hope. I knew in my heart that both Ray and Jim would have urged me to do this, as their first concern was always for my well-being.

Encouraged by the story, I took to recording my own 'strawberry moments' in my journal. To others they might appear quite trivial things, but they helped restore my balance. One day, a friend took me to a lakeside café where we spent an hour watching tiny ducklings waddling along behind their mums – a sight which never fails to cheer my heart.

After that morning shopping with friends — including Nessa and Alison who had travelled some distance to be with me — it was time to set off for the hospital once more. I knew the sights I would see there would unnerve me, but before I left, I recorded that 'strawberry moment' in my journal with these words:

> *My girlfriends were my 'angels' today.*
> *Properly laughed for the first time in ages.*
> *Life can be so bittersweet!*

SYLVIE NICHOLLS

Chapter 8
The Illness Is Not the Person

Love is not love

Which alters when it alteration finds

- William Shakespeare, Sonnet 116

Climbing the steps of the pulpit of a church I was visiting for the first time, I watched as Jim slipped into the back row. Although a practising Catholic, he liked to support me whenever he could. On this day, however, he had sworn me to secrecy over his identity and we had walked in separately. I did not know the reason, but I might have guessed it had something to do with his mischievous sense of humour. As the service ended that day, he had turned to the man next to him in the pew and remarked, 'Well I didn't think much of that preacher...she was rubbish!' Fortunately, he did not allow his unwitting neighbour to squirm for long, whether from horror or embarrassment, and announced, 'Only kidding. That's my missus up there!' When he related this piece of mischief to me my first response was, 'But what if he had agreed with you!' Jim clearly believed that was not a possibility, and I thanked God again for his unwavering support, shown above all in his willingness to follow me round the country to wherever I happened to be stationed as a minister.

SYLVIE NICHOLLS

Jim had been a Catholic lay minister when I first met him, though no one would have labelled him 'religious' in any negative sense of the word. He never pushed his faith on anyone, but was a listening ear if a colleague wanted to chat about God, or ask him what to buy as a christening gift for a relative. It amused him when people made assumptions about my character due to my role. Like the time we were staying in a guest house for a week, with a landlady who loved to engage us in conversation at every opportunity. She was unaware of my work until the last morning of our stay. Jim went down to breakfast before me, and she asked him what I did for a living.

'My wife's a minister,' Jim replied.

'Really? But she seems like a normal person...'

Such memories popped into my mind during one of my long vigils at Jim's bedside. His mind lurched between episodes of confusion and lucidity, but I wanted to be there in moments when the 'old Jim' shone through with clarity. I was conscious of how I was, at the same time, already mourning the person I felt I had lost through this ghastly tumour, whilst trying to appreciate short interludes when I caught glimpses of that vibrant, funny personality once more. 'This is a taste of what it must be like to see someone suffering dementia,' I thought one day. It caused me to feel both admiration and empathy for those I knew who were forced to watch that cruel disease erode the personality of their loved one.

Any person can suffer from an illness. But the illness is not the person. There was so much more to this man than the increasingly haggard, confused visage he presented.

THE TREASURE ON THE SHORE

Something I had always admired about Jim was his ability to tell a good story. He could recall events and personal interactions so clearly, often adding a comical twist. It might be a conversation he had with another fisherman on a riverbank, or about a news item with a colleague at work. If, occasionally, he embellished the facts, it was out of a desire to put a smile on the face of his hearers.

Whenever Jim attended a parents' evening for our son — something he often did alone due to my working most evenings — I could be confident that I would get an account of the proceedings as if I had been there in the room myself. One night, he came home chuckling to inform me that the teacher of seven-year-old Michael had suggested he might like to read a recent piece of work on his part. The class was asked to write a piece entitled, 'My Parents'.

At that time, I was heavily involved in conducting weddings, and sometimes would get an anxious bride or bridegroom calling, as had happened not long before. Jim had answered the phone to one such groom: 'Can I speak to Sylvie? She's marrying me on Saturday!' Jim swiftly replied, 'Oh no, she's not. She's married to me!' At least it broke the ice! Michael had obviously taken note of this, along with my regular absences at evening meetings, but decided to exaggerate things somewhat. He wrote in his account: 'My mum goes out every night and leaves my dad and I on our own...She marries lots of men.' Worse was to come, though.

Michael loved to pop into the room at home where Jim stored his collection of World War One memorabilia, which included pictures of soldiers in uniform, many books on the conflict and items such as antique brass shells. Michael interpreted this in his terms: 'My dad keeps bombs in his room and likes to look at pictures of dead people.' At this stage, Jim registered my look of horror and imminent fear that social services would shortly arrive on our doorstep. But he laughed and said the teacher understood the context and saw the funny side. Much to my relief, the remainder of the essay had praised our parenting skills.

Remembering such antics as I sat by the bedside helped me to remember how the illness is not the person. Jim's humour, when it came, was now flatter, more passive. The threads of storytelling were starting to unravel, requiring too much mental attention to sequence and structure. As I held the hand of the man I had known and loved for twenty-five years, I realised I was also holding our shared history. Within that history, the beauty of his personality still shone through and could be communicated to others. I was the guardian of that light even as his mind grew dimmer. Years after he left this world, I would recollect one of his stories with a friend and Jim would still have the power to light up both our lives again.

THE TREASURE ON THE SHORE

Still You

You're still there.
Behind the vacant stare
You're still there.

You're still You.
Although the mind may dim
The Light shines through.

You're still mine.
Love doesn't alter
When it alteration finds.

SYLVIE NICHOLLS

Chapter 9

When You Haven't Got a Prayer

People can easily assume ministers of religion enjoy some kind of 'hotline' to God. Yet, like any other human being, you can reach a point where you feel you just haven't got a prayer. Even if you are someone who normally has what you think is a healthy prayer life — whether you speak with God formally or informally through the day — anyone may reach a point where they just don't know how or what to pray any more. Then again, you might not be familiar with prayer at all but, in the face of an emergency, may experience an inner prompting to give it a go as something which can't harm and might help. It's like the story of the telephone repairman who told a priest and spiritual guru arguing over the best way to pray: 'The best praying that I ever did was when I was hanging upside down from a telephone pole.'

Sometimes, we are so depleted of physical or emotional energy that the very thought of praying feels too much to contemplate. I reached such a point in the middle of Jim's illness. For a start, I could not believe that thirty years after Ray passed away, I found myself in a similar position: the spectre of imminent death overshadowing us daily. Everything felt too raw, too painful. When I did have a moment to myself, I chose to keep busy with whatever work I could reasonably carry on with, or lose myself in some mundane television programme that didn't require much focused attention.

SYLVIE NICHOLLS

Then, something strange happened. Random numbers began to pop into my head at odd times through the day. The first time it happened, the number came with an inner prompting to look at a Bible. I didn't have any high hopes of making sense of it but decided to look up the Psalm with that number. As I read it, a phrase jumped out at me: 'They will have no fear of bad news; their hearts are steadfast, trusting in the Lord.' *(Psalm 112:7)*. As I read it again, though all other forms of prayer had eluded me, it felt like this was the prayer my heart most wanted to pray at that moment. Over subsequent days, I began to trust the numbers that came to me. Nearly always, there was a word or phrase in the Psalm it referenced which I could relate to, in the light of what I was going through or feeling that day.

All human life is there in the Psalms, ready to give voice to our deepest fears, anger, or sorrow. Sometimes, it would be the words of a heartfelt plea which seemed to speak on my behalf to God, as in Psalm 13.2: 'How long must I wrestle with my thoughts and day after day have sorrow in my heart?' I didn't always accept meekly a phrase brought to my attention. When the words 'delight in the Lord' leapt out at me from Psalm 37, I scrawled in my journal, 'What on earth does this mean amid this pain?' In response to these words, Psalm 113 reminded me: 'He lifts the needy from the ash heap.' I 'wrote back' to God, 'I am right in the middle of an ash heap. The ash is in my throat right now!'

THE TREASURE ON THE SHORE

This kind of inner dialogue at least meant God and I were maintaining a relationship of sorts. Though daily life often didn't make sense, or brought new trauma, I began to recover a sense that God was listening, understood, suffered alongside us and that, above all, He wanted me to feel less alone.

SYLVIE NICHOLLS

THE TREASURE ON THE SHORE

Chapter 10

Behind the Smile

Appearances are often deceiving.

- Aesop

As a trainee journalist, I learned an important lesson about not judging people on appearance alone. I was despatched to interview a local farming couple but got off on totally the wrong foot when I met them by assuming (on looks alone) that they were mother and son. They were man and wife; something the said wife put me right about in very assertive language! I felt doubly foolish since my then fiancé Ray was twenty years older than me. Although Ray looked younger, I thought how mortifying it would have been for someone to mistake me for his daughter.

After Ray became ill, I found myself visiting an elderly widow to take down details for her husband's obituary. Her grief was very raw. I sensed anger simmering beneath the surface of her measured response to my probing questions about the life of the deceased. Suddenly, she lost control and began to loudly accost me. 'You're so young! What can you possibly know about death and what it's like to lose someone?'

Caught off guard by such an outburst, I wanted to yell, 'More than you think! My husband is bed-bound at home, often in pain and with only months left to live!'

67

SYLVIE NICHOLLS

Instead, I bit my tongue, reminding myself that this was not about me and my experience, but about her own grief. I responded as calmly as I could, 'You're right. So, tell me what it is like...'

It has been said that we should try to be kind to each other because we cannot know what battle the other person is fighting at that very moment. I have known so many people who are struggling with serious issues in their lives but on being asked, 'How are you?' will force a smile and respond, 'I'm fine!' Someone said that 'FINE' can stand for 'Feeling In Need of Encouragement'. I have learned to ask the more specific, 'How are you doing today?' The latter might be as much as someone is able to articulate in the midst of long-term pressures.

Sometimes, the person we are seeking to support may not want us to probe too much behind what might be a painted-on smile, but to provide them with a brief respite from living in some reality they might relish the chance to escape from. Jim and I knew such a reprieve on a walk we attempted in the middle of his illness, though the giver of the kindness would have been oblivious to its impact for good upon us. Jim was feeling perhaps too optimistic about being able to walk to a nearby café which, even at his ever-slowing pace, we thought could be managed within ten minutes. I watched with growing concern as this man, who used to outpace me with his long, speedy strides, ambled slowly along beside me. Halfway there, he stalled, so we rested on a convenient bench. A moment later, a car drew up on the road beside us. An elderly lady got out and, glancing over at us sitting on the bench, flashed a beautiful smile as she said, 'hello'.

THE TREASURE ON THE SHORE

For Jim, ever one to strike up conversations with strangers, this was all the encouragement needed. The two of them were soon happily chatting away, and I thanked God for the smile on Jim's face as he regaled her with a couple of his stories. The illness was not referred to. This lovely lady was not to know that the smiling figure before her had looked quite different in appearance before his gruelling treatment began, so she took him simply at face value. As she turned to go, her closing remark was, 'You two look so fit and happy today!' I simply smiled in response, inwardly reflecting on the irony that Jim was very far from fit that day, and I was very far from happy.

SYLVIE NICHOLLS

The Walk

It was such a glorious summer's day —
And the café did not seem that far away.
Ten minutes at most if you took it slow,
And you were oh so keen to go!
You used to stride out so quick and fast,
But now you wondered how far you'd last.
Five minutes in, and your strength was gone:
'Let me rest, my dear, and then we'll go on.'
And there was a bench in just the right place,
So there we sat, as I watched your face
And read the sad question in your eyes:
Was this simple pleasure to be denied?
A car pulled up as we rested there,
And out of the car an old lady emerged,
Who smiled and said, 'What a lovely day!'
And so our journey was further delayed,
For the two of you were soon chatting away.
As she said of her car, 'That has seen better days!'
How I longed for the better days of our past,
For just then each day seemed worse than the last.

THE TREASURE ON THE SHORE

Then I heard her remark as she went on her way:
'You two look so fit and happy today!'
The thought this encounter left with me,
Was just how deceptive appearance could be:
For there, one of us had been inwardly crying
For the other one, who was inwardly dying.

SYLVIE NICHOLLS

THE TREASURE ON THE SHORE

Chapter 11
Things Could Be Worse

One evening in July, during a blessed break from treatment, Jim and I were quietly relaxing at home, watching a DVD of one of his favourite television series. Produced by ITV, it features the heroic adventures of Richard Sharpe (Sean Bean) during the Napoleonic wars. Watching his reactions, I could see how its comforting familiarity was having a soothing effect on Jim, who was so relieved to be home again.

In this particular episode, 'Sharpe's Siege', our hero is shown anticipating a forthcoming battle, knowing it will be incredibly tough. His faithful sidekick, Sergeant Harper, appears and holds out a cup of tea, commenting that things could be an awful lot worse. Sharpe snaps back, 'How the bloody hell could things get worse, Pat?'

'We could be without the cup of tea!'

Jim and I both chuckled at Harper's remark: 'Things could be worse' is a phrase meant with kindly intent, but can rankle with those on the receiving end of such platitudes. Sometimes, there isn't a silver lining, however hard we look for it. Jim was undergoing debilitating bouts of chemotherapy and was enjoying this brief respite. Though suffering short spells of confusion, he was reasonably lucid in between. This was a chance to catch our breath and even contemplate a few days away for Jim to fish and recuperate.

SYLVIE NICHOLLS

We were looking forward to attending our son's graduation in a week's time. As we watched the antics of Richard Sharpe, I comforted myself: 'Yes...things could be worse...'

Within minutes, they got worse.

For once, it wasn't about Jim. The phone rang with a message which shattered our already decimated world. My precious mother, Caroline, had died suddenly. Mum had been in hospital after a fall at home, but there had been no warning signs death was imminent. She lived some distance from us and I had been due to travel to visit her in only two days' time. It would have been the first chance to do so since Christmas, because Jim's illness had prevented a planned Easter visit.

My senses reeling from the news, I recalled our last conversation a fortnight before. It had been 6th July, Mum's birthday. We had spoken of how much we longed to see each other. If I had thought it would be our last conversation, how much more would I have said. Suddenly, my mind flashed back to another 6th July thirty years before: standing by an open grave in the cemetery as Ray's coffin was lowered into it, feeling like a little girl again as I gripped Mum's hand tightly and apologised to her that we were laying him to rest on her 'special day'. She had loved Ray so much. I hadn't found a way to tell her Jim might be dying, too.

I could barely take in the news of her death, coming on top of all we were going through. When I put the phone down and tried to share it with Jim, I scanned his face for any reactions which would mirror what I was feeling;

THE TREASURE ON THE SHORE

shock, anger, disbelief, but his face was a blank canvas. Maybe some part of his brain was frantically searching through its internal filing system to pull out the right response, but failing miserably.

Sometimes, only a hug will do. Not from anyone, but from someone dear to us when we are sad or grieving; especially when we feel we are hanging on to life by our fingertips. This was such a moment. I wanted — needed — a hug from Jim more than anything else in the world that night. But treatment and medication had not only blurred normal powers of comprehension but rendered his body painfully sensitive to touch.

It shocked me that Jim could not process this event on any level. In our 'other life' he would have held me tight, told me everything was going to be all right. As I slumped on to our sofa, I clung to the mildly self-soothing effect of such a fantasy. In our 'other life' we would have shared stories and memories, for I knew how much Mum meant to him. They had such a special bond: Mum adored Jim and found him so easy to talk to; so much so, that when the two of them were together I could barely get a word in edgeways. I would sometimes leave them gossiping past midnight as I retired to bed.

How we would have smiled at such memories, including how Mum would bend the ear of anyone who would listen as to how proud she was that I had gone into the ministry. I would send her CD recordings of my services and she would listen to them over and over (as only a mother would).

SYLVIE NICHOLLS

Jim and I would have chuckled over the fact that, when my mum came to visit us, she was — in the words of an old advert about a kitchen cleaning product — like 'a white tornado'. Eager to make herself useful and aware of my often-frantic working schedule, she would set to with a vengeance. Cleaning and ironing until the house was sparkling and our clothes pristine. At times I felt a bit inadequate as, compared to her standards, mine were definitely lacking! We learned to gratefully accept it as another expression of her love.

None of these lovely reminiscences were possible to be shared with Jim that evening. The few precious days away we longed for would now be spent attending her funeral. Before that, we would manage to get to Michael's graduation, but, inevitably, the day was overshadowed for him too, by the loss of his much-loved nanny. The nanny whom he said 'made the best Yorkshire puddings I've ever eaten'.

Within days, and still with a savage sense of unreality, I was standing in the grounds of a little church as a hearse arrived at the gate ready to discharge my mother's coffin for the service. My sister, Carol, and brother, Bob, stood beside me. Jim was under Michael's watchful eye, already settled in the front row inside the building, not being strong enough to make the short walk up the aisle. As the coffin was carried towards me someone behind me called out: 'She's here!' I felt my legs give way. This was not the meeting I had planned and looked forward to for so long. This time, it was not heavenly angels bearing me up on either side, but earthly ones in the shape of my brother and sister.

THE TREASURE ON THE SHORE

Next to Godliness

My mother died tonight, dear heart,
But you were far away, sweetheart;
Not in distance, but in mind:
The comfort that I longed to find
Within your arms a memory,
Your ravaged body finding even
Gentle touch was just too much.
My tears and grief I could not share
For you were fighting for survival there.

I could not shout and scream with pain,
That I would never see her face again.
That all the things we'd had to bear
Had left no chance of seeing her,
Before she died. No: Instead, I had to wait
To greet her coffin by a churchyard gate.
Her last days had been tough, I knew,
Plagued with worries for us two:
I'd dreaded making a call to say
That another husband had passed away.

SYLVIE NICHOLLS

I know you'd really loved her, dear.

Think how we'd laughed when, every year;

When she came to visit it always seemed

She just loved to cook and iron and clean!

From top to bottom the house she swept:

She made our efforts look inept!

Didn't Jesus talk about houses too?

'And I go to prepare a place for you– '

If I know my mum (and I think I do)

She will find some way to welcome you:

So have no fears, dear: Just follow the light

To the cleanest mansion in paradise!

THE TREASURE ON THE SHORE

Chapter 12

Human Kindness

Remember there's no such thing as a small act of kindness. Every act creates a ripple with no logical end.

- Scott Adams, artist and Cartoonist

'Hi there! Having a good day?' came the enthusiastic greeting of the assistant in the hospital shop where I was buying a snack. It's strange how the most innocent of words, spoken in the wrong context, have the power to wound. No, I was definitely not having a good day. I had come from the bedside of my husband, Jim. He had nearly died that day. It was not information I was ready to share, so I moved aside quickly as the assistant greeted the next customer in similar cheery terms. I wanted to challenge him! 'Is that the right thing for you to say to people in such a place?' Unless we're visiting a new mum in maternity, most people here won't be having a good day. Couldn't you simply say, "How are you doing today?" or "Hi! " But such confrontation requires emotional energy, and I had none left to expend.

When you are in the position of being a carer for someone, whether they are living at home, in a home with a big 'H', or in hospital, there are days when you reach rock bottom and feel incredibly vulnerable as a result.

Such moments were regular occurrences for me over the nine months of Jim's illness; for many carers this can go on for years. When you are in the middle of 'one of those days' it is surprising how the smallest of things can lighten your mood or depress it. I was in receipt of so many small kindnesses shown by friends, who probably did not realise the impact they had at the time.

Jim spent most of his last months in hospital. Anyone who has been in that position will describe how draining it is to spend hour after long hour at the bedside, not to mention being ejected in the middle of your visit with little time or energy to get home and back for the next visiting slot. I was fortunate to have a car and not have to battle with bus timetables. A saving grace was friends who sometimes offered lifts back and forth, keeping up a cheerful banter when I needed it most. Or those who kept me company in some of those 'in between hours', such as Julie, a friend who would drive over to join me in the hospital café for coffee and chat. Her husband has a long-term debilitating condition, so there was so much I didn't have to explain to her about how I was feeling.

Inevitably, there were days when what was happening to Jim would totally knock me off balance. On one such day, I was feeling terribly anxious about unpleasant side-effects he was suffering from chemotherapy. Rather than succumb to the tears welling up in me and risk distressing him further, I decided to take a break for ten minutes, and wondered where I could go to compose myself before returning. Spotting a sign for the hospital chapel, I made my way there, hoping to find a few minutes peace and quiet away from the constant hubbub.

THE TREASURE ON THE SHORE

Just off the chapel entrance was a small prayer room which seemed to be open for just such a purpose. As I went to enter the room, a woman rushed out of the chapel, almost knocking me over. I thought she might have been getting things ready for a service later that day, and felt it was appropriate to check with her that I could sit in the prayer room for a while.

In response, she spoke quite sharply, 'As long as you don't disturb anything in there,' pointing to robes hanging behind the chair, then bustled off on her way. As I flopped into the chair, I reflected on the fact that what I longed for in this place was a little human interaction — someone who might have a few minutes to listen to my recalling the horrors of the hours beforehand. I might then have felt strong enough to return. I did not want to blame the woman I encountered; she was obviously busy and distracted. Yet part of me wished she had paused for a moment and taken notice. I was sure my face told its own story.

It made me think of how we should never underestimate the power of loving gestures, however small or insignificant they may seem. They just might help the recipient get through the day. On that particular day a few kind words, even a brief interaction, would have made such a difference to me.

SYLVIE NICHOLLS

Sanctuary

Today my strength so quickly drained
And I sought a sanctuary from the pain.
So I followed the hospital chapel signs
Towards the refuge I longed to find.
Near the chapel a door was open there,
To a prayer room with a comfy chair.
With the Cross in sight and Bible too:
Yes, I might sit there and pray for you.

Then out of the chapel a woman rushed
Abruptly against my clothes she brushed.
I inquired of her as I caught her eye,
And short and sharp she gave reply:
'May I use this room for quiet prayer?'
- As long you don't disturb anything there!
Then she gestured and gave a pointed stare
To the priestly robes, hanging by the chair.

She sounded so peeved, as if wondering why
Her attention was claimed by this passer-by.

THE TREASURE ON THE SHORE

And she said not a word to ask me why
I was seeking a place to rest or cry:
Then she might have offered to be my friend,
Instead of just warning me not to offend –
Or taken a moment my comfort to seek
And help dry those tears so fresh on my cheek.

I wish she'd just asked if I was OK,
For I was the one most disturbed on that day!
How I wish she had held my hand and prayed
That the last of my strength would not slip away.
Please notice your friends and neighbours today:
If you see a need please don't rush away,
But consider the blessing that you might be
To a human soul, seeking sanctuary...

SYLVIE NICHOLLS

THE TREASURE ON THE SHORE

Chapter 13
Shall We Talk About Death?

'We were decades, still, from a time when a simple Google search would bring up a head-spinning array of charts, statistics and medical explainers that either gave or took away hope.'

- Michelle Obama, Becoming, writing about her father's diagnosis of MS.

When my first husband, Ray, was diagnosed with bladder cancer, he was informed he would likely die within a year. I heard this damning verdict first not from Ray himself, but from my sister, Carol, as I sat at her kitchen table nursing a cup of tea. She had summoned me urgently from work. I do not think Ray could bear to impart such news himself. As much a burden as the disease itself inflicts upon a sufferer, they dread how much it will impact the lives of their loved ones. The next day, Ray came home from the hospital, where he had been admitted for what should have been a simple prostrate operation, and began the long and painful descent towards his demise. There were less treatment options in those days, and he passed away ten months later. Death might have been staring us in the face but we never alluded to it. Out of my earshot, he gave clear instructions to a minister friend about his funeral.

Jim was never told in my hearing, 'This is how long you have got left to live', nor did I ever hear him ask the question. I came to understand how doctors today are very reluctant to quote figures, unless really pressed to do so. It is never an exact science. Certainly, Jim received mostly cheerful optimism from his consultant about the chances of recovery. Yet at the same time we were being warned the treatment was 'very aggressive and life threatening'. I could not help but wonder whether Jim existing in a 'bubble' where he believed he would be well again in six months and able to return to work was that helpful. I had done enough research to know a rosy future was never on the cards and that chemotherapy, followed by weeks of radiotherapy, would likely give him only more months, not years.

In this respect, 'Dr Google' has a lot to answer for. As I imagine is the case for so many, it was the first place I turned once I had a 'label' for this thing threatening to devastate our lives. I mulled over and over in my mind a phrase which had never previously featured in my vocabulary but would now dominate my thoughts: Primary Central Nervous System Lymphoma.

Naturally, one of my first questions was about survival rates: How long could someone live with this thing? One site I visited spelled out how, left untreated, the average survival length after diagnosis would be one-and-a-half months. I reeled from the knowledge that Jim had been only weeks from death. But how many weeks from death was he now? In random moments, I indulged in a weird 'Russian roulette' amongst medical websites.

THE TREASURE ON THE SHORE

I felt pathetically relieved when I found one which seemed to hold out hope of a longer reprieve before the inevitable demise. Those that held more dire prognoses embedded themselves like bullets in my brain. I felt conflicted between wanting to be prepared for the worst, and not wanting to know the worst; drowning under a deluge of fear-inducing facts, whilst clinging to the absurdist of lifebelts. Like when I read, 'People over 60 are more vulnerable and respond less well to treatment.' Surely that meant Jim, at 58 years old, must have a better chance? Whenever I came across phrases like 'doctors cannot predict how long someone will live or whether the cancer will recur' I mentally asserted, 'Of course! Doctors don't know everything! And miracles happen!' They were phrases I had heard others echo, as they sought to cling on to hope in similar circumstances.

I understood the almost constant, frantic trawling of the internet, which so many carers are driven to embark on. We hope to stumble across some new research in the area of disease afflicting our loved one. Some 'miracle cure' that might be accessed by raising funds to take them to a hospital in Europe or America; somewhere where they have been pioneering treatment with amazing results. Sometimes, that search leads somewhere which promises genuine hope. For Jim, I could find no way out.

Having acquired such a plethora of information in the early stages of Jim's illness, I was at a loss to know what to do with it. I was clearer about what not to do with it. In Jim's fragile mental state, a conversation about survival rates seemed an impossible burden, and one he was unlikely to be able to process at any level.

It had already broken his heart to be unable to carry on with the job he loved, supporting students with special needs. Through gruelling bouts of treatment, he was still talking in hopeful terms of returning to the classroom. School staff were expressing how much they and the students were missing him. No doctor was discouraging what seemed to me more and more a forlorn hope.

The realisation that someone's life is likely to end within months, as I knew with regards to Ray and Jim, is like watching a scene from an old movie. Your loved one is strapped to a railway track and a train is fast approaching. As it rushes towards you, you realise there is nothing you can do to help them. No hero is going to suddenly appear and save them, and you are being forced to stand by and watch.

In the role of minister, I had sat at the bedsides of the seriously ill and sometimes felt prompted to have the 'death' conversation – that is, to try (as tactfully as possible) to create an opening so that, should the patient wish to share any thoughts about dying, I could offer a listening ear. The patient would usually say they were relieved to have a conversation with me about things they found intensely hard to raise with their family. But I could never quite bring myself to have the 'death' conversation with Jim. I wanted him to have whatever comfort he might draw from his hope of recovery for as long as possible. If we lived in cloud cuckoo land, sometimes it seemed preferable to the alternative. Death was not so much the elephant in the room, as a gaping pit right in the middle of it, threatening to swallow us both if we ventured too close.

THE TREASURE ON THE SHORE

A couple of months before Jim passed, he would have a conversation about death with a good friend, but I did not hear of it until after he passed. I suppose we had both been inhabiting an illusion, seeking to protect each other from the looming disaster. Perhaps it might have helped us both to acknowledge it.

SYLVIE NICHOLLS

Death and the Doctors

You can tell the ones
In fear of Death:
Their eyes avoid your eyes.
They pretend that all is well.

You can tell the ones
At ease with Death:
They do not give false cheer.
They help you to prepare well.

Chapter 14

Dreams and Visions

But still I dream that somewhere there must be the spirit of child that waits for me.

- Bayard Taylor

When Jim was very sick, I dreamed he had caught a bus which I had just missed. I watched helplessly as the vehicle disappeared in the distance. I cried out after it, desperate for Jim to hear me. Realising I could not stop it by my frantic pleas, I gave up and yelled after it, 'I'll be along later!' I did not need a dream interpreter to tell me this was an image thrown up by my subconscious about the anxiety of being left behind as Jim made his journey into another world where I could not yet follow.

Shortly after Ray died, I had a significant dream which eventually led me to candidate for ministry, so I had long been interested in dreams and visions. A few years before Jim passed, I had written an MA dissertation on the subject of Dreams and Early Methodism. John Wesley, the founder of Methodism, had a remarkably open attitude towards phenomena like dreams; he judged them by their fruits. If a significant dream prompted a change for good in the life and character of the dreamer, Wesley was content to attribute its source to the Divine.

SYLVIE NICHOLLS

During his illness, Jim was the subject of a number of weird and wonderful dreams himself. In one, he handed a substantial sum of money over to his consultant — perhaps a subconscious wish that it would increase his chances of recovery! In the months following his death, Michael had a number of dreams in which he met and interacted with his father. It is not uncommon to dream of lost loved ones. Whether these are actual encounters with spirits in the next realm or imaginary wish fulfilment is something for each dreamer to make up their own mind about, but they usually bring comfort. This was certainly the case in relation to an astonishing vision Jim experienced about a month before he passed.

This vision concerned a child we had lost through early miscarriage. When it happened, we had only been married five months and were living in a flat at Queen's College, Birmingham. I was enjoying my second year of training for ministry. Jim was still on home ground himself, being Birmingham born and bred. The timing seemed perfect. We were both keen to start a family before I took up my first appointment as a deacon and were so excited that even a few months into the pregnancy, we had already decided on names for a boy and a girl.

Our dream came crashing to earth when I was rushed to hospital with severe bleeding. We had no way of knowing whether our baby had been a boy or a girl at that stage, and the loss hit us hard. Miscarriage at an early stage is not at all uncommon, but as anyone suffering a similar loss will know, it is so hard mourning a little soul you have not even had the chance to meet.

THE TREASURE ON THE SHORE

We were heartbroken. Jim told me later how he had paid a visit to the College Chapel alone and railed at God. Little did we know that in later life, both he and our new baby boy, Michael, would lay claim to encountering that child.

When Michael was four years old, Jim would take him for rides on his bicycle, strapped securely into a child seat. On one occasion, Michael began complaining loudly that his dad was sitting too far back on the bike and 'squashing Sam'. This happened several times, and we concluded that 'Sam' must be Michael's imaginary friend. We thought this was rather sweet. Jim decided to play along with the game and ask Michael a few more questions.

'So how old is Sam?' he asked Michael one day.

'Sam is five.'

Another time, Jim asked, 'How is Sam today? Does he like riding on the bike?'

To which Michael replied rather indignantly — as if his dad should know: 'Sam's not a boy! She's a girl! And she's not my friend. She's my sister!'

Jim and I were stunned but also incredibly moved by this revelation. Assuming he was too young to understand, we had never shared any details of the miscarriage with Michael. We had never mentioned to anyone that, had our baby been a girl, we were going to name her Samantha, and she would have been a year older than Michael.

A few months after this incident, Michael stopped mentioning Sam, but he always remembered her. A couple of years later, we overheard someone ask him if he was an only child, and he replied, 'No I'm not. I have a sister.'

At Jim's bedside a month before he died, I noticed his spirits seemed much lighter than usual, so I asked him if anything had happened. He described having a vision in which a young woman had greeted him with the words, 'I've waited a long time to meet you, Dad.' Somehow he knew this was his daughter, Samantha. She had taken him into a room where a lot of people were already present. He had known some of them in this life, but they had died. Others he did not recognise, but he still knew he had some deep connection with them because Samantha was introducing him to each one.

Neither of us was ready to acknowledge that death might be imminent, but as he spoke, I understood how this vision had lessened Jim's fears about it. It was as if he believed all these people would be waiting to greet him when he crossed over. I marvelled at what he told me and could only thank God for the comfort it had brought him.

THE TREASURE ON THE SHORE

Chapter 15

Meltdown

The first day Jim and I met, I could hardly take my eyes off him. It was 11th November. He later joked it was one anniversary he was not likely to forget, with its associations of Remembrance, for the history of the First World War held great fascination for Jim.

We had been pen-pals for a few months, having both joined a Christian friendship group which aimed to link people with similar interests. I first contacted Jim to ask him about his experience with the group because I was very apprehensive about joining and providing my contact details to strangers. Jim seemed the perfect person to contact because he lived over one hundred miles away from me, in Birmingham, so (I reasoned) was unlikely to land on my doorstep uninvited. We hit it off straight away on the phone, but resolved to be only pen-pals, as it seemed impractical to try and manage anything else from such a distance. Letters, not phone calls, we agreed. If we had met in modern times, we might have ended up face-timing every night, but I am so glad that option was not available. Our letters were such a gentle way to get to know each other. Mutual regard blossomed, but we still had no plans to meet, and I was in no hurry to enter any more romantic entanglements.

SYLVIE NICHOLLS

At the beginning of that year, I had broken off an engagement. The wedding was booked to take place on my birthday in July and I had bought a wedding dress in the January sales. But I had begun to have doubts, which I only really admitted to myself the evening before St Valentine's Day, in a heart-to-heart conversation with a pastor friend. I had felt an increasing pull towards candidating for ordained ministry, but my fiancé made clear it would be the end of our relationship if I did so. There were other reasons why I realised we might not be a good match. I felt so guilty and sad when I ended our relationship the next day — on a day when love is traditionally being celebrated. It was not that my fiancé was not a kind, decent man — he was. I was relieved years later to discover he had made a good match himself. But with startling clarity, I realised it would be better to remain on my own than end up with the wrong life partner.

After we parted, I applied to be considered as a candidate for diaconal ministry in the Methodist Church and was summoned to an initial interview in Birmingham on 11th November. On hearing of this, Jim wrote, offering to meet me at New Street Station before the interview and show me the sights of the city afterwards. As we had never set eyes on each other before, I informed him I would be wearing a purple suit and would meet him under the station clock. Any romantic connotations of this arrangement were lost on us before our meeting. Jim was anxious, he told me afterwards, not to accost the wrong woman who happened to be dressed in purple.

THE TREASURE ON THE SHORE

But we caught sight of each other in the crowd and somehow knew we had the right person. Later that day, as we strolled past Birmingham Register Office, Jim pointed out the building and joked: 'That's the Register Office. Will you marry me?'

I replied, 'Thanks. But I don't usually marry men on the first date. Maybe the second or third!'

We doubled up in laughter. That was the moment we acknowledged that we were actually on a date, and that there would likely be more to follow.

On the day we met, I could hardly take my eyes off him. Now, on this day nearly twenty-five years later, I could hardly take my eyes off him again, but for totally different reasons. When Jim had spells at home, he needed to be watched almost constantly. My vigilance had previously saved him from sepsis as I had recognised the early symptoms and rushed him in to hospital for life-saving treatment. The responsibility felt both a privilege and a burden. It made me reflect on the dedication shown by the carers I had known, who must feel like this for years on end, watching over a loved one and never knowing when the next crisis would strike.

I had noticed a severe deterioration in Jim's condition. He could barely get out of bed or stand without suffering the most severe back pain. The week before, his legs had suddenly given way and he had toppled over. I decided to describe his symptoms to a MacMillan nurse over their telephone helpline. She judged him to be at risk and urged me to seek medical help urgently.

SYLVIE NICHOLLS

Both she and I speculated whether the cancer might have spread and be damaging his spine. I recalled what I had previously read about his condition, how cancer cells could grow in the spinal cord as well as the brain. Feeling desperate, I bundled Jim into the car and drove to A&E.

After a wait of several hours, the doctor on duty ran some tests but dismissed my worries as groundless, putting it down to after-effects from his fall. Late that night, we were summarily dismissed from the department. By this time my nerves were so frazzled that, confused by some new roadworks on a nearby roundabout, I managed to turn north instead of south on to the motorway which would have taken us home. It was going to be 13 miles before I could turn round and begin the trek home. Every mile brought with it groans from Jim, squirming in agony on the seat beside me. Eventually neither of us could stand it any longer and we pulled off into a motorway service area. I managed to book a room there for the night and put Jim to bed, bringing some relief. We travelled home the next day.

That day, I wrote a frantic letter appealing for help to our GP, explaining my concerns. The next day he arrived on our doorstep; thank God was my inner response. But what happened next, I could not thank God for. The doctor stood in our dining room, where Jim now laid in bed, and asked a few cursory questions. Pronouncing that this was a case of sciatica, he suggested that I should not write any more letters. As he left, I felt broken and unable to think of anything more I could do. Who would help us now?

THE TREASURE ON THE SHORE

The answer to that came when Jim had to be rushed into hospital a couple of days later. I could only feel relief that whatever was causing this breakdown would be fully investigated now, and slept more soundly that night. I did not realise how much I would need that rest until I visited the next day. Jim was absent from his bed. The ward was bustling as usual, but I could not find anyone to talk to, to even ask where he was.

Finally, I stopped dead in the middle of the long, central corridor of the ward and crumpled, surrendering to the tears I had been holding back for days. That certainly aroused attention. A passing nurse took me to one side and listened to my pathetic pleas. 'I can't find my husband and nobody will tell me where he is!' As I blurted this out, I had a sudden mental flash — Mary standing outside the tomb on Easter Sunday, pleading with the 'gardener' she didn't realise was her risen Lord, after he inquired why she was weeping. Mary's words of 'if you have carried him away, tell me where you have put him, and I will get him' resounded in my mind and captured the crazy longing in my heart to somehow rescue Jim and escape from this place.

The nurse spoke gently enough, not realising her words were triggering an earthquake in my soul. Jim, she explained, was having radiotherapy. Why? Yesterday, she explained, they had found another tumour. This one was on his spine.

'Why hadn't anyone let me know?' I wailed incredulously.

'We thought he would have done that,' came the reply.

SYLVIE NICHOLLS

Once again, I found myself inwardly cursing the fact that a brain tumour patient may be too confused to be able to pass on vital information to the family. But nobody seems to allow for that outside the specialist neurology ward. Jim was virtually bed-bound from that time.

Chapter 16

Thoughts Which Taunt

Visiting my doctor following the death of my first husband Ray, he commented how, in his experience, I was somewhat unusual.

'Why?' I inquired.

'Because you have not asked me questions like: "Could anything more have been done?"'

'You mean such as: "What if you had given him this pill or tried this treatment instead of that?"'

'Yes, that sort of thing.'

I explained that I had not asked such questions because I believed everything that could have been done for Ray had been tried, for better or worse. And that was a comfort.

With Jim, however, doubts lingered — the kind I had heard first-hand from grieving relatives; thoughts that torture the bereaved when at our most vulnerable. There were times when I asked myself, 'Has everything which could be done been done?' Or, 'Is it happening quickly enough?' Even making allowances for the vagaries of the NHS and the limitations of hard-working, often overworked, staff.

Sometimes you read about a parent with a sick child wringing their hands in the midst of a crisis because a health professional has delayed diagnosis, dismissing their instinctive sense that something is badly wrong as some kind of parental hysteria. As we negotiated the hitherto alien world of hospital visits and aggressive treatment regimens, I was probably viewed similarly at times, trying to quietly advocate for Jim when I felt things were not being picked up or dealt with appropriately.

There seems to be special challenges to our health system posed by someone presenting with a brain tumour, which became apparent at almost every stage. When Jim was a patient on wards other than neurology, he suffered greatly from sensitivity to noise and light. Inevitably on a busy cancer ward, there would be constant beeping from some machine or other. I often wished he had been able to have a bed in a quieter corner of a ward, at least away from avoidable noise, such as when his bed was right next to a litter bin with a noisy clanging lid which made him jump each time someone used it. If his over-bed table was moved for any reason, he found himself unable to reach his phone or water jug until I arrived to restore it; the simple adjustment needed to restore the table was sometimes just too much for his brain to process.

Sometimes, Jim would have the benefit of a private side room — but this could be a mixed blessing. On one occasion, I had to block the door to Jim's room to Angela, a friend of ours who was following me in. I had glimpsed a distressing scene before me.

THE TREASURE ON THE SHORE

Jim was lying on the bed naked, having somehow managed to discard both pyjamas and bed covers. He looked so exposed and vulnerable, lying shivering in the draught of an open window. In his confused state, he had no perception of how this looked or how to summon help to remedy it. I felt acute shame on his behalf. It felt as if he was stripped of dignity as well as clothes, and what if I had not arrived to restore both? As I invited our friend, a former nurse, into the room, she raised her hand to her mouth in shock when I explained the reason for the delay.

My faith in the system was tested to the limit time and again. One time, I was on the receiving end of a casual remark, which would have sounded innocent to anyone else, but it crushed my spirit. It happened when Jim was a patient in the rehab unit, soon to be discharged after treatment for secondary tumours on his spine. As I stood in the ward chatting to a member of staff about how he was doing, she casually remarked, 'By the way, he says he's been having headaches. Is there something wrong with his head?' Her question stunned me into silence. Before I could respond, she was called away to a patient's bedside. She did not see me put my head in my hands as a tear coursed down my cheek. I had never felt more helpless or hopeless.

SYLVIE NICHOLLS

Is There Something Wrong with His Head?

Is there something wrong with his head? (She said)
Thank God we were not standing next to your bed!
Is there something wrong with his head?
And her question hung in the air, right there
For rage and shock made me gape and stare,
Is there something wrong with his head?

Is there something wrong with his head? (She said)
He says that his head hurts at times (She said)
Is there something wrong with his head?
Her question had served to strike me dumb
I wanted to scream but it just wouldn't come.
Is there something wrong with his head?

Is there something wrong with his head? (She said)
Did she know why I stood there, shaking with dread?
Is there something wrong with his head?
Then she dashed off to answer a call from a bed
And I cradled my head in my hands as I said:
'Yes! There's something wrong with his head!"

Chapter 17

Checking Out

Email to a friend, two weeks before Jim's death:

Tough week. Respiratory arrest Monday, then heart problems late last night when we were called in and he nearly died again. Stable this morning in coronary care. His mind is getting more confused so communication tricky. Still hoping for nursing home. Love S.

That particular Monday afternoon, I had only popped out of the ward to buy a snack. As I repeatedly pressed the door buzzer to be readmitted, I realised why no one was paying me any heed. Through the clear side panel of the door, I could see, only feet away, the door to the side room where I had left Jim resting peacefully minutes before. Now all was noisy commotion; a rush of staff down the corridor, pushing a large machine in front. I felt like a driver who, following a blaring ambulance, watches anxiously as it turns into their own road and begins inwardly praying 'please don't let it stop at my house'! My breath caught as it did stop at 'our house'! People and machines were crowding into Jim's room, the door shut hard behind them. Was this it? Was my precious husband checking out of the world at this very moment? I could not say how long I stood there, but it was like the surface of my mind was slowly freezing over.

Perhaps I wanted to remain frozen there, my hand next to the buzzer, my face against the glass, not daring to move on to the next moment and what I might have to face within it.

The next thing I remember was a nurse opening the door and gently shepherding me into a small private room. I steeled myself for the worst. Instead, she spoke in almost self-congratulatory tones of how it had taken six people to revive Jim after his collapse — but they had brought him back. However, if such a collapse happened again, they would advise letting him go. I tried to process the meaning of this statement and how I was supposed to feel about it. Should I be ecstatic that he was back in the 'land of the living', or devastated that it it happened again tomorrow, they would let him drift away? My poor loved one had been pummelled back to life in a way which must have caused further trauma to his body. Before very long, he would have to go through a similar process of attempting to depart this life. One which might prove more prolonged and painful for us both.

As I drove home that day, I pondered what I had heard many times from the lips of a newly bereaved person when, for whatever reason, they had not been able to be physically present by the bedside of a loved one when they had drawn their last breath. They were devastated not to be present; some experienced an acute sense of guilt, however unwarranted it appeared to others. Perhaps they had been keeping a long vigil by a hospital bedside but had chosen to take a much-needed break, maybe to travel home to rest or pop to a hospital café.

THE TREASURE ON THE SHORE

They would say with great sadness things such as, 'I was only gone a few minutes. When I got back, he was gone.'

Occasionally, I would have a deeper conversation with a friend about this kind of thing, and we would ponder: Was it just a coincidence? Or was it too hard for that human spirit to leave this mortal coil while their loved one was sitting there, perhaps inwardly begging them to stay? In a final act of love, did they wish to spare them from witnessing their passing? Jim and I had also had such a conversation, long before he became ill. He too was curious over what the answer might be, but we kept an open mind.

That day, it became all too real. Just before this latest drama, I had been sitting by Jim's bedside, both of us enjoying the rare peace and quiet provided by a private room. This was a great relief to me, for I knew how much harsh lighting and background noise affected him and set him on edge. He was not in a mental state where we could have much conversation, but it seemed as if words were not really necessary.

We sat there quite at ease in each other's company. I was conscious of a pervading peace in the room, and Jim seemed more physically comfortable than he had for some time. As the afternoon wore on, I grew tired, so I whispered in his ear that I was going to pop and get a snack from the cafeteria. Within ten minutes, I was back to witness the drama which ensued. I could imagine many in that situation overcome with relief that their loved one had been brought back from the brink. I suddenly realised that Jim might have been making a choice, as far as anyone might be able to, to depart at that moment.

It would have been as 'good' a passing as anyone might have hoped for. It was not that I wanted Jim to go; I did not want him to ever leave, but looking back on the events of that day, I wondered if it would have been a blessing to release him from further suffering.

THE TREASURE ON THE SHORE

Checking Out

You tried to check out, my love, that day.
But they would not – or could not - let you go.

Such a peaceful afternoon we'd spent,
In each other's company content:
The shadows were lengthening outside
Few words: Just a meeting of the eyes.
A quiet room, with lights I'd dimmed,
Shutting them out. Shutting us in...
No noise here to clatter in your ears
Quite cosy: The two of us, in here.

I'd just popped out to get a snack –
'Not long, darling – I will be right back.'
But they would not let me back to you:
Blocked at the door and forced to look through
As machines were summoned to your side
In place of the woman you'd made your bride.

'

SYLVIE NICHOLLS

'Oh yes it took six!' They would proudly say,
To block your departure on that day,
To shake and shock you back to life
And then inform a desperate wife:
'If it happens again, we'd certainly say
It's best if we just let him drift away....'

We'd sometimes pondered this, sweetheart:
Can souls choose the time that they depart?
To save us pain or to give them ease,
They might check out when their loved ones leave...

You tried to check out, my love, that day.
But they would not – or could not - let you go.

THE TREASURE ON THE SHORE

Chapter 18

Seeking Shelter

You matter because you're you, and you matter to the end of your life. We will do all we can not only to help you to die peacefully, but also to live until you die.

- Dame Cicely Saunders, Founder of the Modern Hospice Movement.

I had a rather rude awakening to the hospice movement. It happened during my time training for ministry at Queen's Theological College in Birmingham when I was given the opportunity of a week's chaplaincy placement in a city hospice. Arriving at reception, eager to create a good first impression, I was greeted by a passing member of staff: 'Oh good, you're here — welcome.' She ushered me off to a nearby bathroom, instructing me to administer a bath to the elderly patient waiting within. In my naivety, I assumed I was just being 'dropped in the deep end' and resolved to do as good a job of it as I could manage. Unfortunately, it involved a rather sophisticated hoist system I had no idea how to operate. Thankfully, the patient in question took pity on me and she explained the finer details. We muddled through together, accompanied by a good deal of laughter as we wrestled with an electronic hoist which appeared to have a mind of its own.

Shortly afterwards, a new nursing student on placement turned up at reception, and everyone realised that I, the chaplaincy student, had been mistaken for her. The member of staff profusely apologised while I speculated whether we had saved the nursing student from being assumed to be a chaplain and ushered off to a bedside to pray for a patient. We all saw the funny side and it proved a great icebreaker as I was introduced to other staff.

Many of my preconceptions about such places were challenged during that week, and rightly so. I assumed there would be a pervading mood of misery — far from it. Of course, there was a more serious side but there was much more humour than I expected, from both residents and staff. The care afforded to the patients was exemplary. I admired those who felt called to work in such a setting, for I realised it must be incredibly tough going at times. The Christmas before had been an especially awful time, when several young mothers had passed away only a few weeks before Christmas Day.

On learning the hospice manager was a Christian, I asked her if she had ever lost her faith in the face of such heart-rending circumstances. 'No,' she responded, 'I have never lost my faith. But it has been severely shaken at times.' I could well believe it. As Cicely Saunders is reputed to have said, on hearing that someone had observed a look of love and steel in her picture in the National Portrait Gallery, 'Love and steel: how kind. Anyone doing hospice work will need plenty of both.'

These memories raced through my mind as I watched Jim in the last stages of his illness.

THE TREASURE ON THE SHORE

The hospital could do no more for him, yet he required twenty-four-hour care of a level I would not be able to administer at home. How do you let go and more fully entrust the care of your loved one to others at times like these? I had seen so many church members reach that point, where you recognise you can no longer offer the essential support needed, or it might take a toll on your health if you attempted it. When I had walked alongside others making such decisions, I had sometimes offered words such as 'hard as it is to see your loved one enter residential care, you can now spend what time you can with them as a partner, not a carer'.

I thought back to how Ray had become bed-bound at home some months before he passed. At that point, I realised I had no energy left to look after him and fulfil my part-time job as an editorial assistant on a local newspaper. Bizarrely, when I went to the editor and explained I had to leave to look after Ray full-time, he offered me a pay rise to stay on. Money was tight, but it would have been strange to accept such an offer in the light of Ray's needs. We spent his last months together at home, with little support from outside agencies.

For Jim, a choice was made for me when the hospital needed to free up his bed. It was arranged for me to be ferried round various local nursing homes which currently had vacancies. I had visited enough residential homes over the years to know that their quality varied widely. Staff were usually overworked and underpaid, but those who took pride in their work made such a difference to the lives of those they cared for.

SYLVIE NICHOLLS

In Jim's case, what a fiasco this search became! The man allocated to drive me round couldn't have been nicer, but I could see him, like myself, becoming more discouraged with every rejection we received. Home after home was initially welcoming and enthusiastic, before deciding they could not cope with a brain tumour patient with Jim's specific needs and deteriorating condition. They also expressed surprise at his age (58) as if that alone was a good enough reason for exclusion.

At one home, we were ushered into a bedroom the size of a box room, housing only a single bed and a chair. At least the window looked out on a patch of green countryside which I thought might comfort Jim. Last of all, we visited a Sue Ryder home. This appeared in every way to be the most comfortable and comforting environment in which to spend his last days. Here, at last, they understood neurological conditions and how to ensure his well-being. Our hopes were dashed, though, when they explained that there was simply no room to accept him as a resident. Perhaps when they had built a planned extension? I knew that would be too late. We were weeks away from Christmas, and I could not help contemplating what it must have felt like for the heavily pregnant Mary to be told, 'There is no room at the inn.'

Meanwhile, Jim languished in his hospital ward. Three other men in the ward were in a similar position, in desperate need of release from hospital to home or hospice. Within a short time, each one had passed away. I would arrive to be told by Jim, 'Another one gone!' I shivered at the sight of curtains drawn round the bed of the patient in question.

THE TREASURE ON THE SHORE

Pressing for action, I was told Jim would have to be close to death to be moved to a local hospice. 'How close to death did they mean?' I wondered. Days? Hours?

Finally, I fled to what had always proved a haven for me amongst the chaos: the Macmillan Help Centre based in the hospital. Here, as usual, they sensitively listened to me and offered support as I made my plea. I explained how, as a minister, I did have some awareness about dying, and I believed Jim did not have very long. I just didn't want to walk in one day and find a curtain shroud round his bed; I wanted his last days to be as comfortable as they could be in the circumstances.

Shortly after this conversation, Jim was reassessed and admitted to a local hospice for the remaining days of his life on this earth. St Catherine's Hospice proved a blessed refuge where they cared for me as well as him. In that place, I felt Jim was no longer just a patient, but fully recognised as, and cherished for, the person he had been and still was. Not only because of the family photograph on his bedside, showing him in his prime as a proud father and husband, but in the whole gracious manner of how we were both treated during that week. As soon as he was moved into a quiet, private room, I felt I could breathe again.

SYLVIE NICHOLLS

No room at the inn

You're so weary of hospitals, darling boy;
You just want somewhere to rest your head:
Though they keep telling us that they need your bed,
There is no room at the inn.

They ferry me round the nursing homes,
Where they boast of the treats that you might enjoy:
But when they assess you, my darling boy,
There is no room at the inn!

They say you're too young, with too many needs,
Yet you long for a place that feels like home;
And we know that we cannot cope on our own,
But there's no room at the inn.

Now here is a lovely Sue Ryder Home,
Where they tell me they'd have you like a shot!
But 'til they build an extension they just haven't got
Any room left at the inn.

THE TREASURE ON THE SHORE

Men die around you: One, two, three:
And I now know the signs of death so well:
So I wonder why others can't seem to tell
That you need room at the inn?

You so need a safe place, darling boy -
A hospice room to take your last breaths
But they say that unless you're days from death
There is no room at the inn!

These places of refuge need our support
So we needn't leave anyone out in the cold:
And so no one else need ever be told:
'There is no room at the inn.'

SYLVIE NICHOLLS

Chapter 19
Surprised by Joy

Knowing my heart's best treasure was no more;

That neither present time, nor years unborn

Could to my sight that heavenly face restore.

- From 'Surprised by Joy' by William Wordsworth

During my years as a minister, I have read all manner of books about death and dying, as well as listening to and learning from the personal experiences of those facing such issues. I have read and heard some accounts of how those dying, in their last days, might be able to see things beyond our sight; like visions of loved ones gone before. We might greet such stories with scepticism or optimism, depending on our own experience. I can only speak of mine.

The day before Jim died, in the middle of one of the worst times of my life, I was 'surprised by joy'. Six days earlier, he had moved into the hospice. Unable to utter more than a few words, he remained largely in a semi-conscious state. I knew his pain was under control and was moved by the love extended to both of us. Jim looked so worn and haggard, a contrast to the photograph of the handsome, smiling man I placed by his bedside. He had been through so much; I could not wish his suffering to be prolonged any longer.

I walked into his room that day expecting to see much the same picture of someone hovering on the cusp between life and death. What I saw shocked me — but for different reasons from what I could have expected. Jim was asleep, but the expression on his face might best be described by an unfamiliar word: beatific.

Various dictionary definitions expand its meaning to include words such as, 'rapturous, joyful, ecstatic, seraphic, blissful, serene.' My favourite definition, which seemed to fit best of all, 'imparting holy bliss.'

I watched, entranced, as Jim would now and again raise both of his arms. It looked like a gesture of 'welcome' as if someone had just walked into the room to visit him. Was he hallucinating? I wondered. If so, it must be quite some hallucination to be imparting the joy I could read in his face. It felt like I was standing on holy ground. I knelt down by Jim's bedside, intending to offer a prayer, for it seemed to me as if something was happening in that room beyond human sight or knowledge. As I knelt there, I dared to pray that, if something special was happening, might I be given a glimpse or a taste of it — if only for a moment?

No sooner had I prayed this, than I felt flooded by a force of love so strong I had no words for it. The whole room resounded with its energy, as if transporting me out of one dimension into another. I could sense 'presences' around me, communicating intense peace and comfort to my spirit, though I could not have said who or what they were.

THE TREASURE ON THE SHORE

Then, perhaps only seconds later, I was 'back', gazing at Jim who, judging by the blissful smile on his lips, still seemed to be inhabiting that other dimension, and vastly enjoying the trip. Uttering a prayer of gratitude for what I had experienced, I rose to my feet with a new assurance in my heart. This assurance was that, even if I was not present, Jim was not going to die alone, and, perhaps, (I thought) none of us die alone. Later that day, I bent to kiss Jim on his forehead, whispering in his ear, 'Bye love, see you tomorrow!' Within hours, he would slip the bonds of this world for ever.

SYLVIE NICHOLLS

The Day Before

The day before you left, dear,
Your face in slumber changed:
You looked so young and carefree,
No longer strained by pain.

A smile kept playing on your lips
Like I'd never seen before;
You raised your arms as if to greet
Some visitors at the door.

You had seen our unborn daughter
In a vision that you'd had —
When you'd heard her whisper fondly:
'I'm waiting to meet you, Dad.'

Although I felt like weeping
Your smiles made me laugh instead!
Were angels – or lost loved ones –

THE TREASURE ON THE SHORE

Now gathering round your bed?

I couldn't see what you could see
But I prayed that I might feel
Some semblance of their presence
And know your joy was real.

Then at once it overwhelmed me:
A Love far beyond this world —
And a fleeting sense, my darling boy
Was with our darling girl.

The day before you left, dear,
Did your spirit just take flight?
Then its shell, no longer needed
Simply shut down in the night.

SYLVIE NICHOLLS

Chapter 20
The Day After

Round Robin email, 16th December, 2014

Jim passed to glory this morning 2am.

OK to share news with others.

God bless, Sylvie

There is such a surreal quality to the first dawn after the earthly existence of a loved one is ended. It heralds a new day, but it is a day you wish to opt out of living through. You wake in a world which has stubbornly refused to stop turning merely because one of its inhabitants has vacated their designated space within it. If you have slept at all, you wake to some alternate reality you are not inclined to embrace. The aftershocks come in waves. Violent thoughts assail you: What has happened? What do I do now? Who needs to know? They rush into your mind with an avalanche of raw and conflicting emotions. Relief that one nightmare is over. Rage that it has swept so many dreams away in its wake. Dread of the new nightmare beginning, not just for yourself, but for anyone else whose world is inevitably shattered by this event.

SYLVIE NICHOLLS

I woke in the hospice after a few fitful hours of sleep fuelled by emotional and physical exhaustion. There was sheer bewilderment: Here I was, still alive, but with two dead husbands. A widow once again, thirty years after losing Ray. It was a 'label' I had hoped not to resume wearing until I was a very old lady. How had I even got to this strange bed? My mind struggled to reconfigure the preceding hours. For some reason it flipped back to an incident, when I was six years old, in the playground at primary school. Playing a game of tag with a friend, I tripped over and badly grazed my knee on some gravel. I howled with pain and sat down nearby to recover, hoping the blood would stop trickling and the pain would end. My friend came over and stood gazing curiously at the seeping wound. I thought she was going to sit down beside me and offer sympathy (like a story I would later share with pastoral visitors). Instead, she prodded her finger straight into it, whilst innocently inquiring, 'Does that hurt?' Now, as my mind continued to assault me with images from the hours leading up to this present moment in the hospice, it was as if some great, gaping wound had opened up in my spirit. Someone or something was prodding it over and over, all the time asking, 'Does it hurt?' Surely, they ought to know that it hurt like hell, and stop it.

Bit by bit, I recalled how the previous night, I had travelled home as usual after spending most of the day at Jim's bedside. At about 11 pm I felt an overwhelming urge to contact the hospice.

THE TREASURE ON THE SHORE

As soon as a nurse answered the phone and told me she was standing right outside the door to Jim's room at that very moment, I thought the prompt must mean something. 'Yes, his breathing has changed,' she gently explained, 'you might wish to come back.'

At that time of night, I was able to get there in ten minutes. I was admitted and gently shepherded through the quiet corridors to Jim's room. They had placed a chair by his bedside which I could comfortably stretch out on and hold his hand through his final hours. I was anxious about his laboured breathing but was assured he was being carefully monitored to ensure he was free from pain. As I lay beside him, I prayed and read a Psalm. I thanked him for the life we had shared together, for our son, for all he meant to us both. I told him that, while he might have wanted to save me the pain of being there when he passed over, I would be OK. A little after two in the morning his breath, which had grown increasingly noisy, abruptly ceased. The room was eerily silent.

The nurse who comforted me suggested I did not drive home immediately and showed me to another room where a bed was ready for me to try to get some rest. I chose not to ring home at that hour, assuming our son was fast asleep. I wanted him to have as many hours of rest as possible to steel him for the day ahead. I did not know he was sitting up that night waiting for news. Or that his faithful friends Dan and Joe had stayed and kept a vigil by his side. After I woke, Deacon Ellen travelled through the chilly dawn to be by my side. Tears in her eyes, arms reaching out, hugging me close.

With her wisdom from long experience comforting the bereaved, she did not trail out empty platitudes but was simply there, offering the warmth of a friend's living, loving presence. I soaked her shoulder with my tears.

THE TREASURE ON THE SHORE

The First Dawn

The first dawn without you
I did not want to greet.
The first day without you
I did not want to meet.
But I did wake up,
And could only sob
On the shoulder of my friend
And rage how I wished
I had not woken up
As a widow —
Once again.

SYLVIE NICHOLLS

Chapter 21
Finding my Still

Look deep into nature, and then you will understand everything better.

- Albert Einstein

Around the corner from the house where Jim and I had last lived together was a beautiful park. I had not spent much time there, apart from the odd outing with a younger Michael to enjoy the crazy golf course. When Jim was in the hospital, I got into the habit of taking an early morning walk there each day as a way of off-setting the long hours I would spend sitting immobile by his bed.

At first, it felt an enormous effort to push myself to get out of the house before breakfast, so that I could fit a walk in before I began my morning's work. My mind would throw up all kinds of excuses to linger in bed, churning over anxious imaginings. But as I persisted, as so often happens with these things, these walks became a habit I no longer tried to talk myself out of. They became as natural a part of my morning routine as having a shower or brushing my teeth. What had started feeling like a 'route march' through the woods that I had to get through morphed into a time which featured some small but remarkable spiritual encounters.

SYLVIE NICHOLLS

Encounters with myself, with God and, within all of that, encounters with the whole awfulness of living with someone slowly dying before your eyes. I came to appreciate how such times supplied strength to get though the rest of the day, and they became indispensable. Rain or shine and summer or winter, I would get out there. On the rare occasions when my will to do so deserted me, the whole day felt much heavier, as a result.

Wandering through the woods, I would pass the usual parade of dog walkers; some may have wondered why I had no dog in tow myself and that neither was I jogging along merrily, like the only other early risers in evidence. Sometimes I would find myself completely alone there, free to speak my thoughts and prayers aloud to God without causing alarm to others. On the worst days I would rage at God. But I came to realise what some writers of the Psalms appeared to discover after first pouring out gut-wrenchingly angry rants: that God was somehow still with me, patiently receiving it all. Some days I sensed my spirit collapsing, exhausted into His arms to be gently borne up in ways which defy easy translation. Gradually, I learned to slow down outwardly in pace and inwardly in spirit. To examine and appreciate the intricate pattern on a leaf; to marvel at the perfectly designed bee 'landing strip' on a purple-headed foxglove.

I continued these daily meanderings after Jim died. In mid-winter, the sight of a once beautiful tree, its trunk cruelly cleft in two by a storm, tore at my heart.

THE TREASURE ON THE SHORE

As I gazed at it, a gentle breeze caressed its broken heart and seemed to touch my own, imparting a deep understanding that everything within God's creation is being held and cherished within His love.

Watching a fiercely babbling brook which had been swollen by heavy rainfall, it appeared to me a torrent of tears; not only my own tears of grief but God's tears, poured out upon a hurting world. With the advent of Spring, I observed the relentless arrival of new life whilst I still longed to cling to the old. My attention was drawn to a freshly opened flower. As I marvelled at its beauty, a still, small voice whispered that not only was I meant to live on, but I could be sure that Jim was living on, also.

Nature is so often spoken of as a healing balm whenever we can access it and take time to enjoy it. Whether we believe in a God or not, the beauty of creation seems to comfort our spirit. It did indeed provide a lifeline for me through those dark days and beyond. As I allowed it to minister to me, my frantic spirit stilled. For anyone watching over a loved one through such times, and trying to survive beyond them, it seems vital to discover something to help still our spirit. Different things work for different people, but I know it is a time for being particularly kind towards oneself, discovering whatever nourishes and calms us. We all need to find our 'still'!

SYLVIE NICHOLLS

The Nature of God

I walked in the woods
When you were ill
And, as my frantic spirit stilled,
I listened out for God.

I walked in the woods
When you were dead
To tame the torment in my head,
And listen out for God.

I raged:
If Lazarus from the tomb was freed
Why can't you bring him back to me?
I've nothing left to give!

I wept:
But in the fiercely bubbling brook
Was shown how my tears also shook
The grieving heart of God.

THE TREASURE ON THE SHORE

God spoke!

And as a gentle winter breeze

Caressed a newly broken tree

Told me that I was loved.

God spoke!

And as the freshly opened flower

Hailed spring arriving hour by hour,

Told me we both would live.

SYLVIE NICHOLLS

THE TREASURE ON THE SHORE

Chapter 22

Healed Beyond the World

We never lose our loved ones. They accompany us; they don't disappear from our lives. We are merely in different rooms.

- Paulo Coelho

Ray and I first locked eyes on each other across a table in a small room at a police station. Later, when people asked me where we had met, I had to qualify that scenario by explaining that we were both there as journalists. We were employed by local, rival newspapers and visited the police station most mornings to pore over crime records from the day before, desperately hoping for an elusive 'scoop' a bit more exciting than the theft of a bike.

When we began dating, my mum naturally expressed concern about the 20-year age gap. We had to cope with the usual 'looking for a father figure' inferences. But Ray never seemed much older to me. He was certainly 'young at heart' and my family grew to love him. He was divorced, which meant that when we decided to marry, we trawled round local churches looking for one which would be happy to perform the ceremony. Though not churchgoers, like many people, we liked the idea of being married in a church. Each denomination we approached laid down 'conditions', such as having to attend services or a marriage preparation course first.

But at one, a Baptist church, the minister welcomed us warmly and laid down no conditions. This quiet gentleman of faith made a profound impression on us. So much so, that shortly after marrying we had a conversation, in which Ray said, 'That minister didn't insist on us going to a church service at all, did he?'

'No,' I replied.

'Shall we go along to one of his services, just to thank him?'

'Why not?'

I have often smiled to myself at the irony of that conversation. We went to church the next Sunday and were so moved by the way that minister preached, we kept on going.

Now, in the seventh year of our married life, Ray was languishing in bed at home, slowly and painfully dying from bladder cancer. Before his illness, we had still been regularly attending a local Baptist church, but Ray was far more committed to God than me. Faith for me was more a matter of habit than heart. One day, a good friend of his visited and took a seat by his bedside. I was climbing the stairs with refreshments when I overheard Ray attempting to persuade his friend about the merits of having faith. He was clearly not having much success.

'I'll believe in your God when he heals you!' retorted his friend. I noted the underlying current of anger in his voice for what he perceived Ray was going through.

'But what if that healing only happens beyond this world?' replied Ray, calmly.

THE TREASURE ON THE SHORE

His friend was silent. Neither he, nor indeed I, were open to such a view. When someone you love stands on the cusp of life and death and whatever may or may not lie beyond, any words of comfort can sound like hollow platitudes. You want that person to focus on living right here, right now, with you, for as long as they possibly can.

Listening to his friend's challenge, I understood why he would cast such a bargain out to the universe. How many of us, at moments of deep suffering for loved ones or ourselves, promise similar favours in return for the healing we so desperately crave. Yet, within a short time, my attitude to God would dramatically change, despite God not delivering the kind of miracle we all prayed and hoped for.

One day I was preparing lunch when I heard Ray cry out urgently. I dashed upstairs, expecting the worst. Instead, Ray looked as chuffed as if the Angel Gabriel himself had just popped his head round the door to say, 'Hello'. He gestured excitedly to the wall opposite his bed.

'Look at that!' he exclaimed. Look at what? I wondered. The only thing I could see on the wall were two small intersecting shafts of light, roughly forming the shape of a cross; a mere trick of the light, I assumed. I fiddled with the curtains, but the outline stubbornly remained in place. Ray was entranced! This puzzled me. Ray was such a practical, down-to-earth man, not easily given to flights of fancy. A man who loved developing new skills and who usually became quite proficient at whatever he turned his hand to whether training as an accountant, working as a photographer, or winning trophies in archery and table-tennis.

He switched jobs and hobbies on a regular basis, so when he said he felt led to begin training as a lay preacher in the Baptist church, I assumed it was just another hobby he would eventually lose interest in.

There was also, what even I as a somewhat 'token Christian' could see, was a major stumbling block for any would-be preacher. Immersing himself in his theological tomes and scribbling away at sermons, Ray said he had no problem with the concept of God at all. But the whole idea of Jesus being both human and divine, dying on a Cross to save the world? He acknowledged he wasn't totally convinced, but hoped his training would overcome doubt. His studies so captivated him that he even tried to persuade me to join in. 'Why don't you try this? You could be a preacher!'

My indignant reply: 'There is no way on earth I am ever going to do that!' Words I have eaten many times since. A few years later, studying for my own local preacher exams, I would discover how the founder of Methodism, John Wesley, had a crisis of faith prior to his famous conversion experience. Confiding in his good friend, Peter Bohler, that he felt he should stop preaching altogether because he had clearly not got enough faith himself, Bohler wisely advised, 'Preach faith till you have it; and then, because you have it, you will preach faith.' I realised Ray had much the same attitude.

Now, just a couple of years after he began his training, here he was, housebound, bed-bound, with every reason to doubt God's existence at all — yet intrigued by a mysterious cross of light.

THE TREASURE ON THE SHORE

The fuzzy outline faded as the day wore on, but a few days later I was summoned again with a cry of 'It's back! Come and see!'

'That's lovely, darling,' I replied. Still sceptical, I was happy to indulge him, because the comfort it brought him comforted me.

A few days later, Ray made (to my ears) an odd request. He asked me to buy a small wooden cross to place on the wall where the cross of light had appeared. Off I went to two Christian bookshops, where I was surprised to find neither had a single wooden cross left in stock. Reluctant to let Ray down, I bought some green cardboard and crafted a simple three dimensional cross. I thought he might laugh at my efforts, but Ray was delighted. The makeshift green cardboard cross took pride of place on the wall opposite his bed. From then, there were moments when I would come upstairs and pause for a moment in the doorway, observing Ray looking very intently at that cross. There was such an expression of peace on his face as he gazed upon it. Then one day he asked me, 'Do you think I'm going mad, love?'

'Why? What's going on?' I responded apprehensively.

'I'm asking that cross questions, and it's giving me answers!'

When I look back, how I wish I had asked Ray more about these 'answers'; but at the time I thought it must be some sort of weird hallucination. What I could not explain was how Ray's views about Jesus and the meaning of the Cross were being transformed.

SYLVIE NICHOLLS

He began to believe that Christ was there alongside him in his sufferings and was helping him to endure them. By contrast, I had only a superficial faith, which did not seem that relevant to daily living. I still could not reconcile the idea of a loving God with the agonies I was forced to watch my husband enduring daily due to his illness. At night, he would wake up three or four times screaming in pain and in need of personal care. This meant both of us were physically exhausted most of the time. We managed to get overnight nursing support for only a single night, and I slept through the night for the first time in months. It was just as well, for early next morning the nurse had to summon a doctor urgently. Downstairs, the doctor delivered a shocking assessment. He believed the cancer had spread elsewhere in Ray's body. He gently explained that should Ray wake up from his current semi-conscious state, the pain could well feel unbearable and he could do little to prevent it. His concern was that Ray was putting up such a fight he might linger in this pathetic state for up to a fortnight. Nowadays, the right hospice care would have served to manage his pain and ease his transition, but nothing like that was available for us.

I was devastated by this news. Ray had been through horrendous suffering, but he had hoped that, when the end came, it would be quick and peaceful. I could not believe he might be denied this last mercy, and I experienced what I can only describe as my spirit shattering with grief and pain. I raged internally at God. Rushing back upstairs, I sat on the end of the bed gazing at my husband of seven years.

THE TREASURE ON THE SHORE

As anger continued to consume me, I jerked round, planning to confront this God symbolised by a green cardboard cross on the wall opposite. As I did so, I cried out from the very depths of my being three distinct words: 'Oh! My! God!'

What I saw in that moment shook my world. A perfect cross of light appeared right underneath the cardboard cross. It did not have the jaggedly outline of the original cross, which I had always assumed was a trick of the light. This was a sharply defined cross of shining white light. I knew there was no logical explanation for this cross. Alongside this vision, an all-consuming sense of peace pervaded my entire being. An assurance resounded deep in my spirit, communicating against all evidence to the contrary. 'It is going to be alright.'

Time stood still. I could not say if I sat there seconds or minutes but I had no doubt about what I was seeing. Then, the cross of light had gone — but the intense assurance it had communicated remained with me. So much so, that I dashed downstairs and announced to my mother, who had just arrived. 'It's going to be alright, Mum. It's going to be alright!' My mother told me later she assumed the strain of the day had caused me to lose my senses. In fact, I felt I had found my senses.

Shortly after the doctor left, Ray's condition took a sudden turn for the worse. He did not wake up again. I spent his last hours sitting by his bedside with a family friend. We reminisced, with laughter at times: about his life and all he meant to so many people. I understood later that hearing may be the last sense to go.

I like to think Ray would have been comforted both by our presence and our mood as he peacefully made his transition into the next life. As I sat holding his hand, there came a moment when I turned to our friend and said, 'He's gone.' There was no obvious sign that he had departed this life; just the strangest, fleeting awareness that the person I loved was no longer lying there on his sickbed but standing in the room beside us. The nurse, who had been waiting downstairs, came back in and confirmed what I already knew.

The inevitable dark waves of grief engulfed me afterwards, but I would never forget the 'peace beyond all understanding' which carried me through that day. That marked the beginning of a whole new relationship between God and myself, and it has been quite a journey. Thirty years later, as I recovered from another devastating loss, it helped me view Jim's situation in a different light: He had been healed beyond this world too.

THE TREASURE ON THE SHORE

Chapter 23

Where's my Happy Ending?

'God hasn't done anything for David,' people are now beginning to say. 'We've prayed and prayed, and nothing has happened at all.'

- David Watson, Fear No Evil.

David Watson was an English Anglican priest, an internationally renowned and much-loved preacher and writer. At the age of 50, David died from bowel cancer just a few weeks after writing the final pages of his book. No one could have been prayed for more fervently. The same year as he died — 1984 — Ray had passed away, and now Jim was gone. I had lost two husbands who were both Christians and for whom a great deal of prayer had been offered on their behalf. I knew in each case that there were some people who felt their deaths meant their prayers had not 'worked.' Of course, I have read books in which people have described miraculous recovery from life-threatening conditions. Against all the odds they recovered, crediting God for their healing. Such books can be inspiring to read, but I have sometimes pondered about the person who has passionately prayed for healing, for themselves or a loved one, and it has not been a happy ending. I have listened to Christians agonising over such negative outcomes: Have I not prayed enough or well enough? Were there not enough people praying?

145

SYLVIE NICHOLLS

If it were that simple (I mused to myself) our churches would be full of people wanting to ensure access to such 'divine life insurance' whenever tragedy struck.

Prayer is something the most hard-line atheist might end up resorting to when faced with terrible suffering. Something in our spirit tries to tune in to something, or someone, greater than ourselves; to some power we hope has more control over events than we could ever have. Crashing disappointment and disillusionment can follow if we think our efforts have fallen on deaf ears, or no ears at all, when our petitions appear to go unanswered.

When you have spent most of your life preaching that God is all powerful, what do you say to the person who is forced to look on helplessly as the person they love diminishes before their eyes? As they rage or weep about the fact that however fervent their prayers and those of others, it seems God has not chosen to restore their loved one to health. When it becomes personal like this, we are stumped to understand what God is up to. At different times, we may resort to cajoling, raging at, bargaining with, badgering God. If we had any kind of relationship with God before the crisis, it is likely to go through a sea change for better or worse.

The arguments behind why God intervenes, or not, have been extensively rehearsed. In traumatic times, they are likely to be about as much use to the one hearing them as a friend who, attempting to offer me words of comfort at my first husband Ray's funeral, blurted out, 'Don't worry. You're young enough to marry again!'

THE TREASURE ON THE SHORE

Which is about as sensitive as urging a young, bereaved mother who has lost a baby that they can go on to have another child.

Church members had shared with me the ways in which their faith had sustained them through times of crises. I had often heard it said, 'I would never have got through this without God. How do people survive without faith?' I am sure we can look around our world and see many examples, maybe within the circle of our own friends and family, of people surviving horrendous experiences with courage and dignity, but who would not profess to having any kind of faith. For many practising Christians or followers of other faiths, however, our worst times may also be times when faith proves its worth and our image of the one we worship is enriched and enlarged.

Perhaps, because my own faith had chiefly been forged in the furnace of suffering, I never believed in a God who would simply stop bad things happening to me. Rather, I learned to trust God as one who, when the bad stuff happened, would prove to be a source of strength and comfort. When I was at a low ebb during Jim's illness, out of the blue, I would feel suddenly comforted and wonder whether someone was praying for us at that very moment. I learned to recognise and thank God for all those moments when I believed that prayers offered on our behalf were actually 'working' to sustain us. Once, when I paused to thank God in prayer for such moments, I felt I heard His voice whisper, 'I may not always supply what you want. But I will provide what you need.'

SYLVIE NICHOLLS

Before he died, David Watson had such a powerful revelation of divine love that he had no fear of what lay ahead. Both Ray and Jim experienced similar revelations: Ray through the 'green cross' on the wall and Jim through an intensely comforting vision. What, I reflected later, were all of these things if not answers to prayers?

THE TREASURE ON THE SHORE

Chapter 24

To Tell or Not To Tell

'To tell or not to tell?' was often the question when Jim was ill. A dilemma which sooner or later must be faced. It is not so much about whether to share with relatives or friends the bare facts of an illness, for it may soon become common knowledge that someone is sick. Rather, how much detail do we wish to share or, indeed, should we share concerning the course of that illness? When training pastoral visitors, I had stressed how not everyone we hear of who is ill wants their details widely shared, and confidentiality must always be respected. What someone shares with a prayer group may not be something they want to be read out to all on a Sunday morning.

The matter is further complicated when someone suffers an illness which induces intermittent bouts of lucidity and confusion; a state anyone with a loved one suffering from dementia understands all too well. The matter of how much to tell, and when, becomes increasingly messy. Our nearest and dearest are usually those we agonise over most, regarding how much to share, and when. When I realised how serious Jim's illness was, I worried about the impact upon our wider family, including Jim's sister, Margaret, and brother, Anthony. Then there was my elderly mother and our son. My mother was very close to Jim, who had lost his own mother. She had already shared in the pain of losing another son-in-law she loved when I was in my twenties.

SYLVIE NICHOLLS

All this meant I tried to cushion her from the whole truth of what was happening to Jim on his worst days, whilst hyping up the slightest glimmer of hope. Most of all, I could not bear the thought that there would likely come a day, not that far off, when I would have to tell her I was a widow once again. I recognised that my mother, like any good parent, longed to do anything she could to prevent us suffering, but equally felt powerless to do so. Of course, I did not know then that she was going to predecease Jim by five months.

A similar dilemma presented itself in relation to our son, who turned 21 shortly after his father was diagnosed. Jim had lost his own father when he was 20. After a relationship which had held some friction, he felt he and his dad were developing a much stronger, adult-to-adult relationship when he died suddenly. I was conscious that myself — and Jim in more composed moments — were trying our best to shield Michael from the more unwholesome details of his illness and treatment; such as the fact that the chemo he received was of the most aggressive type they could offer a patient. We did not want Michael to have to carry a greater burden than he already was whilst trying to complete his degree dissertation.

In the years after Jim passed, Michael and I sometimes discussed this issue. He expressed regret that there had not been an opportunity to have a 'final conversation' of the 'taking leave' type one might have hoped for. By the time there seemed to be a need for it, Jim was too confused in mind to partake of it.

THE TREASURE ON THE SHORE

Naturally, for Jim, it was a conversation he would have found extraordinarily difficult. After the loss of his own father, it would have broken his heart to contemplate not being there for Michael in years to come. I, for my part, spoke to Michael about some guilt I felt that, perhaps, we had tried to shield him too much and should have shared more of the details, however gruesome.

In the middle of one of these chats, Michael surprised me by responding with a teasing hint of irony. 'Yes, Mum, but if you had, perhaps I'd be sitting here today saying I wish you hadn't shared so much detail!' We had come to that place where we both recognised there is no easy template to follow. Each situation is different, without any real way of knowing if the decisions we make are the right call at the time. The hope must be that where mistakes are made, or where others may resent the way in which we make certain decisions, that tolerance may be demonstrated, forgiveness offered and accepted and mercy shown. For as the saying goes, 'We are only human!'

SYLVIE NICHOLLS

Searching...

My spirit roamed abroad tonight
And restless wandered on,
Refusing to accept the truth
That you had truly gone.

My spirit sought to break the bonds
Which clamp it to this earth
And tried to soar to heaven's door
From whence it had its birth.

Once there it might have heard your voice
Or glimpsed your lovely face,
For sometimes memory threatens to
Eliminate all trace.

But my spirit couldn't break its bonds
Nor reclaim your company,
And faced within its black despair
Its own Gethsemane.

THE TREASURE ON THE SHORE

Then from the effort it collapsed
Exhausted at the cross,
And spent itself in one who knows
The depths of pain and loss.

My spirit roamed abroad tonight
But, cornered round with love,
At last gave up its frantic fight —
Locked in the arms of God.

SYLVIE NICHOLLS

Chapter 25

Could I Have Done More?

The kind of questions which haunted me after Jim died were not just, 'Could more have been done?' but 'Could I have done more?' Could I have spoken out more on his behalf? Upheld his cause more strongly, protested more vehemently?

I relived those times when his life hung in the balance. Most of all, I would revisit the moment a doctor had dismissed my concerns, resulting in a delay to treatment for the spinal tumour which robbed Jim of his mobility. Doctors are not superhuman and can make mistakes, but the manner in which I had been treated wounded me. Whenever I described his response to others, they expressed sentiments such as, 'I would have given that doctor what for' or 'I wouldn't have been fobbed off like that.' To those reading this who have known such moments, when it has felt like you up against the world, with little energy left to fight not for yourself but for a suffering loved one, there is no need to explain what I felt. But I was still left pondering. Should I have fought Jim's corner and demanded action that day, or taken him back to A&E myself?

Sometimes, I asked myself whether, if I had been the patient, Jim would have kicked up a greater fuss on my behalf. I was fairly sure he would have. We were quite different personalities, but seemed to complement each other.

Our son, as a teenager, used to joke that if we are supposed to learn from our parents how to behave, he was going to grow up a mixed-up kid.

'Why?' I inquired, keen to improve on what were obviously our parental limitations. 'Well,' grinned Michael, 'if we're in the car and another driver cuts us up, dad behaves as if he wants to kill them, you act as if you want to take them aside and ask if they're having a bad day.' I laughed at the accuracy of Michael's observation. It was not that his dad was always looking for a fight — at work he had been termed a 'gentle giant' who showed endless patience with the students he helped to teach. But he was not one to shy away from a confrontation if he felt there was an injustice involved. On the other hand, I was a mediator, who would make allowances and try to understand what was going on underneath the surface behaviour. His dad would be shouting at the offending driver with a few expletives thrown in for good measure. By contrast, if the same thing happened when I was driving Michael to school, he would hear his mum say with rather less decibels, 'That wasn't a very nice thing to do.' On this point, I did decide to fight my corner with Michael, responding that I trusted he would grow up not mixed-up but well balanced, somewhere between those two extremes!

So, yes, I challenged myself: if Jim felt I was being treated unfairly, he would certainly have been the white knight defending my honour and my dignity however he could. But I was not him.

THE TREASURE ON THE SHORE

Throughout his illness, true to character, I kept biting my tongue and making allowances; endless allowances, convincing myself that surely staff must be terribly overworked or under-resourced to not be paying enough attention to things I thought obvious. That may have been true to an extent, and there will have been times when my perception may have been flawed. But how do you find peace when you believe, rightly or wrongly, that mistakes have been made which have caused a loved one greater suffering; and, equally, when you think you might have made mistakes yourself? We must find our own answers. Some will channel their anger into legal action, others will accept the shortcomings of the system whilst continuing to rage inwardly at it. The person of faith may cry out to God for justice. For me, I write about it, in the hope that somewhere, a weary doctor may pause and speak kinder, less harsh words to a worried relative. That somewhere, someone experiencing similar feelings of helplessness may not feel quite so alone. That somewhere, noticing that an exhausted carer has run out of the will or energy to fight for the right treatment for a loved one, someone may step forward to champion their cause on their behalf. There are already champions like this in the world who have often come through great suffering themselves, but been brave enough to challenge injustice and speak up for the voiceless. They inspire us, as the Bible teaches, to keep on finding ways to bring some good out of the worst times of our lives.

Eventually, I came to a place where I could begin to accept what I might view as my own shortcomings in the matter, and to offer myself forgiveness for them — partly due to my faith that God wished to offer me the same, partly because I believed Jim was now in a better, wiser place and would not wish me to carry the burden of 'what if' any longer.

Chapter 26

Parting With Possessions

There comes a point where you have to begin to let go of items which may have been used, perhaps cherished, by a loved one but which you can no longer justify holding on to. After Jim passed, I stood in our garage surveying a great mass of fishing equipment — rods, nets, canvas shelters — and wondered what on earth to do with it all. I thought back to when our son was about nine years old and decided he would like to try his hand at fishing. We took him to a venue set up with ponds designed for the purpose of encouraging young people to take up the sport. These were extremely well stocked with lots of small fish a child could happily catch regularly under careful adult supervision.

Away from that tailor-made experience, Michael soon realised fishing required much time and patience, and decided it was not for him. But Jim was now 'hooked'. He would regularly escape at weekends or holidays to some quiet fishing haven where he would patiently sit for hours awaiting that often elusive 'bite'. He found it wonderfully relaxing and calming to his spirit, and told me it was on a quiet fishing bank that he felt closest to God.

I had heard from the bereaved how hard it can be to let things go, because the simplest items have associated memories almost embedded into them. It may trigger a fear of losing the memories along with the object.

SYLVIE NICHOLLS

Living through this myself helped me appreciate why people sometimes make 'shrines' of left-behind belongings, even keeping them in familiar places in familiar rooms. Yet I knew, too, that finding a way to release such things back into the world is another step through the wilderness of grief, despite the wilderness feeling a bit like a minefield. As if one wrong step, taken hastily or in the wrong direction, would result in everything blowing up in your face.

When I discovered there was a charity which collected fishing equipment to provide much needed relaxation for soldiers returning from active service overseas, I thought I had found an ideal solution. The day of collection came when I realised something: if you have arranged for someone, from a charity or elsewhere, to collect what you need to discard, you may still want to scream as they do so. 'Yes, go ahead, take it! Someone else can have it or cherish it now. But please, please remember this: to me that isn't just a guitar; that isn't just a football shirt; that isn't just a...'

I wanted to scream like that as the kind man carried the fishing gear to his vehicle. I didn't scream out loud of course, I think he would have made a swift exit in the face of that onslaught. But, inwardly, I was screaming. The rods were going to a cause I knew would be close to Jim's heart. Yet my heart seemed to tremble and shrink as each rod was loaded into the back of that car. What helped me settle in the days afterwards was the knowledge that others would receive benefit from the use of these objects, in a way which I knew would have delighted Jim.

THE TREASURE ON THE SHORE

Similarly, his hundreds of World War One history books were donated to a group, which loaned such books to its members and to schools. Sometimes, the gift offered to others may simply be the donation of our loved one's clothes to a charity shop, which is no less heart-rending to negotiate. It means so much when someone gently draws alongside us in such moments and acknowledges in a few kind words the cost to us of parting with these precious things, for which we have become temporary custodian.

Not everything needs to be released back into the world. Today, I still have a 'memory shelf' in a spare room, on which reside some small items which serve to especially remind Michael and myself of Jim's life and loves — including a football scarf in the colours of Birmingham City.

SYLVIE NICHOLLS

The Rod

It's just a simple fishing rod
And yet, much more you see:
Sweet memories of summer days
Come flooding back to me.

How often in some lake it went,
Bait dangling from its tip,
Then you would wait so patiently
Until the float would dip.

Just sitting by the water side
Your joy was plain to see
I'd sometimes sit, and read a book
And keep you company.

It's just a simple fishing rod
A pole and hook and line:
And yet it brought to you and me
That precious gift of time.

THE TREASURE ON THE SHORE

And on that rod, you'd told me how
One early morn you'd stared
And marvelled as a kingfisher
Had briefly rested there!

It's just a simple fishing rod —
But sometimes, you had said,
You'd felt God's presence drawing near
Right by the water's edge.

And though it tears my heart in two
To watch it leave today
I'll keep such memories in my mind
And send it on its way.

It isn't just a fishing rod!
But now, my darling boy,
I think how you'd be thrilled to know
It's bringing others joy.

SYLVIE NICHOLLS

THE TREASURE ON THE SHORE

Chapter 27

Life After Life

Many of us crave some reassurance that the life of our loved one will continue after death in some sphere of being. If we have a faith which holds out the promise of an afterlife, that may be a comfort to us. In conducting many funerals over the years, I have always checked with a relative beforehand whether the deceased themselves believed in a life to come, so that in any eulogy I would not attribute opinions to them they would not have wished to own in this life. Mostly, even if they had not professed religious faith themselves, they held the hope of a glorious reunion with loved ones gone before. Something in the human spirit tells us there must be more to life than this earthly existence.

Before I became a minister, I was visiting an elderly widow, hoping to offer some support in the sudden loss of her husband. As we chatted, she suddenly exclaimed, 'You don't think I'm going mad, do you?' I sought some context for this remark. 'Well, I sometimes think I can feel him, still around me.' At that moment I felt a distinct fluttering sensation on my cheek, like a kiss. I felt prompted to offer, but not without some hesitation, 'This might sound strange but have you ever felt him...kiss you?' 'Yes!' she responded.

'Here, on the cheek?' I ventured, pointing to my own cheek.

'That's the very place! How did you know?'

SYLVIE NICHOLLS

I explained the sensation I had felt — though in truth, I could barely explain it at all. Her own experience of such phenomena ceased after a couple of weeks. Over the years, I have sometimes heard similar stories from the bereaved. These have included unexplained electrical disturbances in the home after a death; a pet acting in strange ways; the appearance of a robin or butterfly in an odd context. Again, these are usually fleeting occurrences. We each have our own opinions about such experiences, as to whether we reckon they are real or imagined, but they tend to be very comforting to the bereaved.

One of my experiences following the death of Ray was our Doberman dog acting strangely. I would catch her staring intently at a corner of the room where he used to sit as if she was seeing something or someone. I noted it but did not try to explain it.

The week after Jim's death, just before Christmas, brought its own helping of electrical disturbance in our home, particularly lights suddenly dimming with no apparent cause. I pondered such things but tried not to take them too seriously, even joking with my son, 'Your dad said hello again today!' My son had not been present when this had happened; he was happy enough to indulge me, but clearly sceptical about it all.

All this took on an added poignancy when, a few weeks later, he was meeting with a friend in a local pub. She had also suffered a bereavement, so they were commiserating with each other.

THE TREASURE ON THE SHORE

He shared my take on the flickering lights, chuckling with his friend at the thought that I should interpret it as his dad dropping in to say hello. Both were stunned when at that moment, the light over where they were sitting momentarily dimmed. Michael laughed and said, 'Oh no, I know what my mum's going to say now!'

A few months later, Michael and I were standing in the cemetery where Jim's ashes were being interred. A square memorial stone was propped up by the plot ready to be lowered on to it. As my colleague Phil read out words of Scripture, a beautiful white butterfly suddenly appeared and landed on the slab. I had not seen any butterflies yet that season and could not help but smile as it rested there during the reading — a small visual reminder of life and hope.

Then, the butterfly took off and landed in a nearby hedge, very close to my son's shoulder. He too stared at it in wonder. As the stone was lowered, the butterfly took off again. We lived only a short distance away and I watched as it flew off into the distance, in what I knew was the direction of our house. When we arrived home shortly afterwards, there was a white butterfly fluttering round the bushes in our garden. As I marvelled at it, I had a vivid recollection of Jim's laughing visage and could not help but smile in response.

Was it the same lovely creature we saw in the cemetery? I chose to believe it was, bidding a final farewell. Others might assess such events as 'Godincidence' or coincidence, as meaningful or meaningless, but the appearance of that butterfly made a heavy day feel lighter.

In the end, we must trust our own instincts as to how we choose to interpret such events. For me, I believe that God has a hand in finding sometimes incredible ways to comfort us when we need it most.

THE TREASURE ON THE SHORE

Where did you go to my darling?

Where did you go to my darling?
Such words whirl around in my head:
But I'm not recollecting the living,
Just those whom we choose to call 'dead'.

This graveyard's a place to remember —
Where I'll leave you a rose and a cross,
Yet I know that the ashes interred here
Are not all that remains after loss.

For I sensed in that fluttering presence,
Which was just pausing here for a while:
An arm placed around our son's shoulder
And your laughter, inviting my smile.

SYLVIE NICHOLLS

Chapter 28
The Precious Gift of Presence

The friend who can be silent with us in a moment of despair or confusion, who can stay with us in an hour of grief and bereavement, who can tolerate not knowing... not healing, not curing... that is a friend who cares.

- Henri Nouwen

When I was pregnant with my son, I got out of bed one morning and collapsed, doubled up in pain. Jim got me to a doctor, who diagnosed a dose of adult colic. He then rang his workplace to get permission to stay with me, explaining 'my wife has a chronic case of colic'. On returning to work next day, he began to feel the amount of sympathy he was receiving was rather out of proportion to the event. To great amusement all round, he discovered the power of Chinese whispers had turned his message of the day before into the rather more serious 'my wife is a chronic alcoholic'.

Unfortunately, baby Michael seemed to inherit a tendency towards colic. At two years old, he went through a particularly severe bout. Night after night, Jim and I would take turns walking the floor with his little baby head resting on our shoulder, wailing pitifully. Nothing seemed to help. He screamed with pain, would have a brief respite and then scream again.

SYLVIE NICHOLLS

Parents never feel so helpless as when they can't make something better for their child, whether it relates to them being bullied at school or suffering a bout of illness.

As I held Michael in my arms on one such night, feeling the depths of his suffering resound through my being, sure I was not making the least bit of difference to it at all, I asked God for help. Michael's wailing did not cease, but I suddenly felt deeply comforted, as if strong arms were around me and holding me, even as I held him. In that moment, I sensed God imparting something of His comforting presence to me. Along with it came awareness that, just by being there with Michael, sharing in his suffering, I was somehow making a difference for him, too.

As a student minister, I sat by a hospital bed and held the hand of a dying man as his wife sat the other side holding his other hand. We sat there together for some time in silence. I did not feel any compulsion to fill it. It felt complete, almost holy. As I got up to take my leave, his wife looked at me and said with great emphasis: 'Thank you!' Such experiences, walking alongside people going through all kinds of crises, taught me how we should never underestimate the power of presence — of simply being there, alongside someone in life's painful moments. Taking the cue from them as to whether their need is to talk or sit in silence, to say many words or few.

Ray, who had passed away after a long, painful struggle with bladder cancer, had spent his last months bedridden at home. As his illness worsened, so visits from friends dropped off at an alarming rate.

THE TREASURE ON THE SHORE

Granted, his emaciated appearance was not pleasant to behold, but his personality remained intact, relishing a good conversation and a laugh almost up to the end. People didn't know what to say to us once it was obvious there would be no happy ending. Yet, I realised if they had simply come and tolerated sitting for even a short time by the bedside — talked with Ray when he was awake, talked with me when he was asleep — then both they and us would have been blessed by it. If we can learn to better tolerate our own feelings of helplessness or discomfort, to still our mind's restless wanderings, any one of us can be a blessing to another human being in their darkest hours. To all those who, in lots of different ways, watched with Jim and I through such hours, we owe a great debt of gratitude.

There is a poignant episode in the gospels where Jesus, the shadow of the cross looming and aware of the terrible fate which awaits him, prays in the Garden of Gethsemane. Revealing his vulnerability, he confides in his disciples that his soul is 'overwhelmed with sorrow' and asks them to 'stay here and keep watch with me'. Despite several appeals from Jesus, his friends just can't seem to stay awake and be 'there' for him. Perhaps it was just too much for them to think that the person they loved might not be with them much longer, and they took refuge, like so many of us might, in denial.

Watch with Me

> *Then he returned to his disciples and found them sleeping. 'Couldn't you men keep watch with me for one hour?'he asked Peter.*
>
> ***(Matthew 26:40)***

'Just watch with me one hour,' he said:

It was not a lot to ask...

Sadly, His disciples were not

Equal to the task.

For none of them could bear to watch

What just might be the end,

Or contemplate a life without

Their teacher and their friend.

THE TREASURE ON THE SHORE

Could we watch with a friend in need

And their discomfort share —

Though it may cost us dearly

To stay faithful, sitting there?

'Just watch with me one hour,' he says:

For then, your whole life through,

If ever you have need of me,

I will come and watch with you.

(Dedicated to Dan and Joe, who sat and watched with Michael through the night his dad passed away)

SYLVIE NICHOLLS

Chapter 29

Starting From Here

In a remote part of Ireland, a tourist who was hopelessly lost stopped his car and inquired of a passing farmer how he could best get to his destination. The farmer hesitated for a moment before responding: 'Well if I were you, I wouldn't start from here...'

One of the hardest lessons I have had to learn is that the life I shared with a person I knew and loved had gone. That even if my life afterwards resembled a crumbling pile of rubble, I had to begin the process of rebuilding, and I could only 'start from here'.

I don't know the source of that story, but I was born in Northern Ireland and appreciate the pragmatic Irish sense of humour running through it. The punchline became something of a theme for me in the years just after the loss of Jim, when the tides of grief still threatened to pull me under. The tourist could have rebuked the farmer, 'What do you mean? I can only start from here!' I came to understand how too much introspection sapped my energy to deal with what was right in front of me. It was like standing at a crossroads where one of the signs pointed forward stating 'New life ahead' but finding myself stubbornly fixated on the sign, which pointed the way I had come: 'Old life behind', tempting me to mentally rush off in that direction.

Any survivor of loss can attest how the process of rebuilding life again, without a significant other, can be exhausting. We feel like we are losing our way. In such moments, however much I wanted to be in a different place from where I found myself, I would pause and recite the mantra, 'I can only start from here!' 'Here' might be somewhere I did not wish to be, and certainly did not wish to be without Jim, but it was nonetheless a starting point — the beginning of what was to come. I had to carefully examine my surroundings, however rough the terrain, and get my bearings. I had to find any signposts that would allow me to start from where I was, but also give me some sense that I was going somewhere.

It is natural to wish the lost person back again and wonder what things would be like if they were here. But if we spend too much time revisiting the land of our past, it depletes us of energy in the present. Each of us can only start from here when it comes to the story of the rest of our lives.

'Here' may well not be where we want to be, being acutely aware of the absence of someone precious, and how the 'rules' of the universe we inhabit have altered as a result; for instance, in changed relationships with those who have been mutual friends prior to a loss. Newly single, we may feel like the 'odd one out' in groups of couples. But whatever adjustments we are forced to make, we may do a disservice to both our loved one and ourselves if we do not strive for some acceptance of where we are today and, therefore, where we can realistically go from here.

THE TREASURE ON THE SHORE

'Starting from here' does not mean we forget the past. Indeed, it is so important to revisit it at times, recall memories of our loved ones and share them with others when we can. I love to share memories of Jim with our son, as we chuckle together over some of his antics or speculate, 'What would dad have said to that driver who just cut in on us?'

Of course, it can be a dilemma for the bereaved as to how much we can talk about a loved one, especially when in a new romantic relationship. Jim was a very loving husband, but I know he found it difficult when, for instance, we would go somewhere and I would mention I had been there with Ray. It was only when he lost his own brother, Ged, that he realised how important it is to be able to talk about someone we have lost in order to keep their memory alive. He apologised for any times when he might have reacted negatively to my recollections. I never resented Jim for this, though I did wish I had more friends who had known Ray. In any new relationship, it is important to be sensitive and respectful to each other about these things. For my part, I am so grateful for the opportunity of having Michael, family members and friends with whom to chat and remember Jim's life and character.

For those seeking to support the bereaved, we obviously have to take our cue from each person as to how much they wish to share, but there is wisdom in these words from Elizabeth Edwards, regardless of the age or relationship of the person being mourned:

'

179

'If you know someone who has lost a child, and you're afraid to mention them because you think you might make them sad by reminding them that they died — you're not reminding them. They didn't forget they died. What you're reminding them of is that you remembered that they lived, and that is a great gift.'

For the bereaved, we may enjoy revisiting the past but have to guard against getting bogged down there. We use the experience of travelling already gained to plot a course ahead, albeit a different course from what we had imagined, but one which will not lead us endlessly round and round in circles. It is a tribute to our loved one each time we find the resolve to live better and more fully because they lived and loved us.

But I have also learned that you can't start from where someone else thinks you should be. In the years following a loss, you may be in a place where you feel you are coming back to life, emerging from the darkness, beginning to find hope in life again. Or you may feel more like you are falling deeper into the darkness 'not waving but drowning'. In the latter case, others may tire of trying to keep you afloat, or they may make you feel 'you should be over it by now'. But you know where you are and you can only start from where you are, not where anyone else thinks you should be. It is important to show love and mercy towards yourself.

THE TREASURE ON THE SHORE

Having trained as a counsellor, I am a strong advocate of its value in providing a safe, supportive space in which to process experiences and emotions. It is not for everyone, but working with a good counsellor certainly made a difference for me. There is help out there. There are people who will listen without judging. There are counsellors who know how important it is that you are allowed to start from where you are. There are support groups full of people who know you are stuck somewhere because that's where they're stuck, or have been stuck, too. Together, you feel a bit stronger finding a way forward.

And so it proved for me. Over time, I could bear to see a retired couple walking hand in hand round a park and no longer feel compelled to imagine it was Jim and myself, evoking both envy and rage that it never could be. Instead, I could begin to feel a measure of joy in their joy. Then, I realised, I had made a start.

SYLVIE NICHOLLS

Start from Here

It seems I have to travel
Through an unfamiliar land —
Though I wish my life could start from
Anywhere but where I am!

In my mind I've often travelled
Back before we parted ways
But I know that is a journey
Which could dominate my days.

I'm resisting moving forward;
Hesitating, racked with fear,
Yet some quiet voice is urging:
'You can start again from here.'

'When it feels like too much effort
Just let go, and let me steer;
You know that I can help you
To begin again from here.'

THE TREASURE ON THE SHORE

I can only start from here:
In my heart you're always near
But my spirit does acknowledge
I can only start from here.

SYLVIE NICHOLLS

Chapter 30
Love After Loss

"We come to love not by finding a perfect person, but by learning to see an imperfect person perfectly."

- Sam Keen, To Love and Be Loved

I have heard all kinds of reasons why someone may not wish to embark on a new romantic relationship after the loss of a partner. Some are fortunate to find companions to share outings with, and desire nothing more. Others say they could never contemplate matrimony with another person after their loss. If a relationship has been troubled, they may be, understandably, wary of committing themselves again. Once, while buying flowers for a sick friend, I was chatting with the florist about how it must be hard knowing the right thing to say to the bereaved when they placed orders with her. She smiled and said, 'Recently, I was offering some words of sympathy to a widow. She stopped me and said, "No need for any of that. He was a horrible person!"'

Her words reminded me of how hard it is for those who are left with very mixed feelings about a relationship they have shared, which has now ended in death. We can never know, as the saying goes, what goes on behind closed doors. Sometimes a person may be grieving for the relationship they wish they'd had with the other person, rather than the one they did have.

I realised, again, how in seeking to support the bereaved, we should make no assumptions about the grief they are carrying, but rather be concerned to provide a safe space to express it in whatever way they choose. Equally, someone experiencing grief after a divorce might need space to mourn what was both precious and difficult for them in the relationship, without feeling in any way judged for the outcome.

We may be wary for different reasons if we have enjoyed a very good relationship. A friend in her 50s, who had been happily married but widowed for five years, told me, 'I'd never marry again.'

'Why?' I asked.

'I'd never find anyone like him,' came her reply.

She proceeded to describe in detail her husband's specific qualities: his sharp sense of humour; their many mutual interests; even their love for the same movies. At the end of the conversation, I was inclined to agree with her in the sense that she was not likely to meet someone just like him. While I respected her choice, I felt sad that such a lovely person had closed her mind to any chance of a loving relationship with someone else. Someone who would not be the same, but might have their own admirable qualities.

Widowed for a second time, I recalled that conversation and understood it more deeply. No, I was not going to meet someone just like Jim. He would confess to not being 'perfect' (who of us is?) but I missed terribly his capacity for storytelling and ability to make me laugh. Whilst part of me would always mourn his absence and

THE TREASURE ON THE SHORE

the loss of such attributes, I could see the danger of getting sucked into a vortex of past memories which could potentially drain the colour out of any new experiences I might share with someone else. Someone who might not be 'like' Jim, but might be perfectly likeable — even loveable — in their own right. Naturally, I had doubts, among them a reluctance to place myself in a position where I might have to watch anyone else going through the kind of suffering Ray and Jim had endured. It felt much safer to stick to friends/companions without potential complications. After a few years, though, I came to understand that such fears were not a good enough reason for me to avoid a serious relationship, should I be fortunate enough to meet someone. While it would undoubtedly feel like a risk, God had long ago taught me not to be afraid of taking a risk.

Few of us escape the pain of bereavement. As Her Majesty Queen Elizabeth the Second once remarked, 'Grief is the price we pay for love.' As I look back on my life, I realise how much the experience of grief appears at first a wasteland, a barren shore, which is not likely to yield anything of value going forward. Over time, when we can bear to examine it a little more closely, we may start to uncover some treasure which can enrich our lives as we move forward. The treasure will be different for each of us. It might be a life lesson we are grateful for (such as my new appreciation of nature) although we might wish we could have learned the lesson any other way!

It might be the simple recognition that we have been able to survive the worst thing we thought could happen to us and have discovered the will and courage inside ourselves to embrace hope, resolving not to be 'a victim of the world' but 'an adventurer in search of treasure'. If we can discover our own treasure, and maybe use it to help another find theirs, it will be to the eternal memory of the one we have loved, and — for a time — lost.

As Terri Irwin, widow of Steve Irwin, puts it: 'Grief is never something you get over. You don't wake up one morning and say, "I've conquered that; now I'm moving on." It's something that walks beside you every day. And if you can learn how to manage it and honour the person that you miss, you can take something that is incredibly sad and have some form of positivity.'

Epilogue

You will be whole again but you will never be the same.

- Elizabeth Kubler Ross

On Christmas Eve 2020, I drove myself into the car park of the church where I had worked for so many years. This time, I was not there to lead a service. My son, Michael, opened the car door, grinned and offered his arm ready to walk me down the aisle. As he did so, those funny words he had written in his school essay 20 years before — 'My mum marries lots of men!' — popped into my head again and made me smile. That day, I was going to be married for a third time, to Robert, a local history author and church organist.

Happening in the midst of a worldwide pandemic, there were only four other people present besides ourselves: Michael, Robert's two sons, and the presiding minister, affectionately known as 'Reverend Phil', the same colleague and friend who had come across me weeping in the church during Jim's illness. Phil had also lovingly conducted Jim's funeral service alongside Father Jonathan, Jim's priest at the local Catholic Church, where Jim had been a member. I knew he would be so happy for us both today.

SYLVIE NICHOLLS

As I entered the church for a very different ceremony than what I had imagined, my heart ached that I could not share the joy of that day with the rest of my family, as well as with so many people who had supported and prayed for Jim and I during that awful time. That included many church members who would have loved to have been there to celebrate with us. Instead, everyone was wondering how long we would have to go on living with the dreaded Covid; how many more lives would be lost, with people denied the chance to sit at the side of a loved one as they departed this life?

That morning, I had not been able to face putting on the fancy wedding outfit I had picked out a few months prior to what should have been our wedding day in September, had Covid not put paid to it. The dress remained closeted in its white plastic dust cover, perched on the edge of a wardrobe. In an online service, I had even used a photograph of it hanging there to illustrate how many of those listening must have known similar sadness and disappointments. Cancelled celebrations, weddings, birthdays, anniversaries, or seasonal celebrations, including Christmas, when families would traditionally gather. Now, here I was, on my third wedding day, without the presence of so many I longed to celebrate with. So, I decided to hold on to the dress until we could arrange a wedding blessing at a future date. Instead, I opted to wear exactly the same outfit I had worn on my first date with Robert: black trousers, red jumper, cosy, but smart, cardigan. I mused to myself that there must be few brides who had worn the same outfit on both those occasions!

THE TREASURE ON THE SHORE

'You look fabulous!' Robert exclaimed as I joined him at the front of the church that day. I smiled at the memory this evoked. Although we had spoken a number of times on the phone before our first date three years before, those were the first words he had said to me on that occasion, too.

After the ceremony, Robert and I posed behind a beautiful Advent wreath, as our sons snapped photos on their phones. New lockdown rules meant we had to abandon a planned meal out with our guests as well as a mini-break honeymoon, settling instead for a Chinese takeaway for two. But six years and eight days after losing Jim, the season of Christmas would at last become a source of happier memories.

Getting married was a new beginning for me, as was retirement, which followed seven months later. Moving out of the church-owned manse into a new home with Robert, I came across the journal I had written during Jim's illness. I am not normally a 'journal' person, but writing things down at the time, including poems, had helped me survive. Now I would have more time and space to reflect on that time, and on my life as a whole.

Robert has proved incredibly patient listening to my reminiscences as this book unfolded. One day, I had been describing to him the kind of person I had been during my marriage to Ray. For instance, despite an early career in journalism, I had been quite a shy person. Bereavement inevitably impacts our personality and changes us, in great ways or small... for better or worse. Caring for Ray during his illness, alongside the experience of God's grace after he died, had transformed my personality.

SYLVIE NICHOLLS

So much so, that I found I had no fear of public speaking when I felt called to be a local preacher in the Methodist Church. As I shared this, Robert began to chuckle. An image had popped into his head about what might happen if he also made the journey to heaven before me. He could picture a bench where he would join Ray and Jim, chatting together about their years spent by my side. 'I think,' said Robert, 'we might come to the conclusion that we had been married to three different women!'

I could see his point...

THE TREASURE ON THE SHORE

About the Author

In almost thirty years as a Methodist minister, Sylvie Nicholls has specialised in pastoral counselling, with extensive experience conducting funerals, supporting the bereaved and training others in pastoral care. Recently retired, she continues to serve as a pastoral supervisor for lay and ordained ministers.

Sylvie began her working life as a journalist. Her qualifications include the Queen's Diploma in Theology, Cliff College Certificate in Coaching, Diploma in Pastoral Counselling (Nottingham) and MA in Mission & Emerging Church (Manchester, 2011).

Growing up in Northern Ireland, Sylvie's interest in poetry began when, aged 16, she wrote a poem about the Irish conflict which was published in national newspapers in the UK and abroad. She has also had two short stories, including a poem, published in the 'Chicken Soup for the Soul' anthology series. One of these is an account of the life-changing dream referred to in chapter 14. This dream is also referenced in a chapter by Bob Haden in Dreams That Change Our Lives: *A Publication of The International Association for the Study of Dreams* by Robert J. Hoss, Robert P. Gongloff, et al. (Chiron, 2017).

Sylvie has been widowed twice, first at the age of 28, and has an adult son, Michael. She enjoys long walks in the beautiful Lancashire countryside with her husband, Robert, as well as any opportunity to dance.

SYLVIE NICHOLLS

Previous publications:

S. Phillips, 'The Rope' in Chicken Soup for the Soul — Dreams and Premonitions: *101 Amazing Stories of Miracles, Divine Intervention, and Insight* by Amy Newmark and Kelly Sullivan Walden (Chicken Soup for the Soul, 2015)

S. Phillips, 'Samantha' in Chicken Soup for the Soul — Messages from Heaven and Other Miracles: *101 Stories of Angels, Answered Prayers, and Love That Doesn't Die'* by Amy Newmark. (Chicken Soup for the Soul, 2019)

Printed in Great Britain
by Amazon